Happy Relationships at Home, Work & Play

Happy Relationships at Home, Work & Play

Lucy Beresford

 **Professional**

McGraw-Hill Education
McGraw-Hill House
Shoppenhangers Road
Maidenhead
Berkshire
England
SL6 2QL

and Two Penn Plaza, New York, NY 10121-2289, USA

First published 2013

A catalogue record of this book is available from the British Library

ISBN-13: 978-0-07-714591-0 (pb)
ISBN-10: 0-07-714591-7 (pb)
eISBN: 978-0-07-714591-0

Library of Congress Cataloging-in-Publication Data
CIP data applied for

Typesetting and e-book compilations by
RefineCatch Limited, Bungay, Suffolk
Printed by Bell & Bain Ltd., Glasgow

The *McGraw·Hill* Companies

"What is so brilliant about Happy Relationships is that by showing us the simple premise that healthy relationships are as much about valuing and respecting ourselves, as it is about valuing and respecting others, Lucy Beresford offers easy-to-understand advice on how we can all improve and enjoy better relationships, whether with friends, family, work colleagues or our partners."

Jo Hemmings, celebrity and behavioural psychologist,
Psychologist on ITV's Daybreak

"Happy Relationships is THE handbook for the 21st century mortal. With 'top tips', case studies and elegant writing from Lucy Beresford, the challenge of modern living is unpicked. Lucy addresses a myriad of human relationships from dealing with the office letch to the complicated world of social media. Eminently readable Happy Relationships is a book that will end up on everybody's shelf."

Jeni Barnett, TV & Radio Presenter

"Lucy Beresford understands the complexities of human relationships better than anyone and explains how to fix them with clarity, wisdom and warmth."

Clare Longrigg, Editor, Psychologies

"We tend to think that partner love is the key relationship in our life, but all the research shows that we need good relationships with a variety of people - friends, family, colleagues - to be truly fulfilled. Now at last there is a book that addresses all these pairings and suggests ways to make them happy and productive. As an agony aunt I receive many letters from readers who want support in their various relationships; I now know which book they should read!"

Susan Quilliam, agony aunt, relationship coach and co-author of
The Joy of Sex

For Jemima, Harvey, Martha and Anna

Contents

About the Author

Lucy Beresford is a novelist, psychotherapist, and broadcaster. She works in private practice and at The Priory Hospital Roehampton and The London Psychiatry Centre. She is also the agony aunt for *Psychologies* magazine and appears regularly on national and international television and radio, talking about mental health and wellbeing. Her first novel, *Something I'm Not*, was published by Duckworth. She has also had several short stories published and recorded for audio. She is currently working on her second novel, set in a psychiatric clinic in India.

Names and biographical details throughout this book have been changed for reasons of confidentiality

Acknowledgements

A huge thank you to the many people who have enriched my life and whose wisdom, one way or another, has found its way onto these pages, including:

Virginia Whetter, for numerous Whetterisms

Christine Campbell, Romey Chapman, John Costello, and Beverley Archdale, for clinical nourishment

My brilliant colleagues and friends at The Priory Hospital Roehampton and *Psychologies* magazine for teaching me so much

Laurel Remington, for being the best writing support ever

Thomas Johansen, for a mindful intervention

Zeeshan Tayyeb, for all things technological

Margaret and Chris Schofield, for opening their arms

Grace Dugdale, Den Patrick, and Beccy Reese, for keeping me on track

And Sally Willson and Karolina Siudzinska Barba, for keeping me sane

Special thanks go to my wonderful agent Juliet Pickering for her endless warmth, wisdom, and integrity, to my editor Monika Lee for her fabulous positive energy, to both for their fierce commitment to the book, and to all at McGraw-Hill who have helped usher it onto the shelves.

And above all, to Guy, for keeping the flame alight.

Introduction

When you think about relationships, what springs to mind? Does your heart soar to reflect on your family putting a smile on your face at the start of the day, the colleagues you enjoy working with, the friends you care about and who bring out the best in you? Or, do you think of tangles and knots? Resentments or feuds? Errors in communication? Or feeling misunderstood? All over the world friends are falling out, colleagues seethe with unspoken conflicts, and families limp along trying to function the best they can.

How can this be? In the art of trying to get along with other people we have, we might argue, literally thousands of years of practice. We are, after all, exquisitely relational creatures. From the moment we are born, we rely on others for our survival. Later, we learn about life by observing and copying others, not just in terms of tasks – eating food, cleaning our teeth, crossing the road – but also in terms of our behaviour and coping strategies. Whether it's our parents, our classmates, our colleagues or our friends, from conception onwards we exist in relation to others in the world. *Relationships are the mood music of our lives.*

And yet it is often those very same relationships that go on to give us the most agony in life. Life is full of stresses, and as Jean-Paul Sartre put it: to be human is to be anxious. We worry about our health, our career, our weight, our wrinkles. But eavesdrop now on conversations in the pub, on the bus, in your office, in the street, and you'll find there's always someone talking about their latest relationship dilemma.

Or read any agony aunt or photo-story column in the press and you will realize that the majority of the queries are about relationships. These are the narratives of our lives, which we long to see explained and improved. Even the worlds of politics, finance, business, and entertainment are today more often examined with reference to the personalities involved and whether or not certain individuals get on.

And the chances are, if you're reading this book, you've had similar conversations of your own – even if only in your head. My experience in my clinical consulting room and writing my agony aunt column is that for the majority of us there is at least one relationship in our lives – different for each of us, of course – which we wish beyond measure would give us less grief, give us more fulfilment or at least function more smoothly. Yet despite (or perhaps because of) thousands of years of copying each other, we still find relationships a minefield.

One of the reasons why relationships are such a minefield is because deep down we know that relationships are so vital for our wellbeing. They matter *that* much. If the worst happens and all else goes – if we lose the job, the money, the house, even the precious cache of photos or letters – our relationships and our memories of those relationships can make all the difference. They can help get us back on an even keel, they can bring out the best in us, and they can give us the potent strength which comes from feeling supported. We long for the peace a good relationship brings. So how on earth can we stop getting them wrong and start getting them right?

One clue is that we're individuals as much as we're relational creatures. We exist in groups but we're also sole traders. We all have different needs for intimacy, communication, and 'alone-time', just as we all have different childhoods, life experiences, talents, weaknesses, and dreams. Relationships invite the assumption that one template is perfect for everyone, and then repeatedly ridicule this notion by introducing us to new people with different histories, different needs, different templates.

Relationships become complicated precisely because we exist in relation to another person. We might call this person 'The Other'. Our perspective of a situation or event is not always the same as theirs. And then there's a crucial, additional complication to this dynamic, which is that there are always two of us in the relationship with The Other: the part of us that is aware of what we do, and the part of us that does things without realizing it. We might call these 'our conscious' and 'our unconscious'. Our conscious self wants a partner; our unconscious self remembers earlier hurts and is terrified. Our conscious self wants to be a good parent; our unconscious self envies our kids or their opportunities, or is afraid of rejection by them. Our conscious self wants a secure job with a reliable income; our unconscious is terrified of feeling trapped or bullied. Our conscious self wants a best friend; our unconscious self wants to be always in control.

To complicate matters, the twenty-first century has seen the arrival of something that originally looked like it might help facilitate fulfilling relationships: social media. And in some ways, the explosion of Facebook, Twitter, emailing, and texting has had enormous positive influences on how we conduct relationships. But it has also increased the complications. Our relationship skills are weakening. We can hide behind social media accounts and avatars to avoid having authentic one-to-one relationships with real people. And our ability to read non-verbal cues such as body language or facial expressions can diminish. As a result, we struggle in those situations where real one-to-one interaction is essential.

One of the key things that this book will try to show is that *our difficulties in relationships will always say as much about us as they do about The Other*. Unwittingly, we sabotage our relationships because of our own fears and hang-ups. The inner child lurks in all of us, capable of hijacking our emotional responses to certain situations. When relationships flounder or cause us distress, and especially when we find ourselves complaining endlessly about a friend to everyone else, we need to take a step back and see our part in that relationship.

Understanding where our hurt or fear or neediness comes from is the first step in helping us weaken their hold over us in the present. Knowing ourselves better enables us to be fulfilled in our relationships, including the hopefully passionate, exciting, challenging, and rewarding life-long relationship with ourselves. As a result, our relationships will be better able to breathe, we will develop unconditional acceptance for others and ourselves, and our friendships will become so much more fulfilling.

Working at ourselves and our relationships might sound daunting, but the upside is so rewarding – not least because relationship dilemmas can become draining. Relationship issues cover all sorts of terrain and affect male, female, gay, straight, young, old, rich, and poor alike. No-one is immune: How can I deal with my panicking boss? Why is my mother horrid to my new wife? How can I get my step-daughters to like my baby? What can I do about my toxic friend? How can my wife and I maintain access to our grandson? What can I do about my controlling sister-in-law? How can I help my friend who's had a stillbirth? How can I like myself more and improve my self-esteem?

Unravelling the ideas and psychology behind these and other relationship quandaries can answer big life questions for us all. True, there are some people who seem to be more skilled at interpersonal relationships. In my experience, this isn't just down to lucky gifts from the gods or even down to a particular type of temperament, but because such people deploy ways of interacting with others that are successful. They value their relationships and they invest time in them. They're always looking for ways to make them work.

But above all, *they value and respect themselves.* They retain a sense of who they are, or at least who they are trying to become (to some extent the whole of our lives is just one long process of 'becoming'). And they operate in a way which acknowledges that boundaried sense of self. After all, the best relationships – romantic or otherwise – work best when we exist in relation to The Other but are not distant or fused.

In this book, I shall be exploring relationships to show that, by knowing ourselves better, we can start to improve our interpersonal relationships with others. And I borrow from the psychological truth that we learn by copying. Exploring the relationships of others is a rich resource. Reading the examples and case histories in this book showing others struggling with their relationships with parents, siblings, lovers, old friends, in-laws or colleagues, will I hope inspire you to resolve your own personal dilemmas and experience more fulfilling relationships.

Will those relationships be happy ones? Well, happiness means different things to different people. My idea of a person in whose company I'm happy almost certainly differs from the person you're imagining right now. That's because happiness is subjective. It's an elusive concept. Happiness is also not especially permanent. We cannot live life on a permanent upward trajectory. Happy Ever After is the stuff only of fairytales.

And yet we seem obsessed nowadays in pursuing happiness at all costs. We panic if we aren't permanently happy, and over-medicate to imagine we can be. We are in danger of turning the ordinary ups and downs of daily life into a sickness. If we're unhappy, we want quick fixes. We avoid taking responsibility for our lives and instead blame everyone or everything else.

More achievable is an ongoing contentment, a warm glow whenever we think of someone or something – in other words, a good energy. A relationship that puts us in a good mood, that gives us strength or pleasure. And above all, a relationship that is fulfilling, that brings out the best in us, even if all we're doing with that person is sitting at a bus stop when the bus is delayed.

In this book, you will discover how some relationships can bring great joy, and how some can function better than they do. Others have past their sell-by-date, giving us permission to leave them behind. This book will help you decide which ones are working for you and which ones aren't.

You've read up to here, which means that (on some slightly post-modern level) you and I are in a relationship now. Author and reader. One human being to another. You're in a relationship with the Me in this book. You may end up shouting at the page, scribbling notes in the margin, underlining a sentence, tweeting or emailing me suggestions for improvements, throwing the book in the bin (or at least giving it to the nearest charity shop!), recommending it to a friend, or keeping it on your shelf for future reference.

And you're in a living relationship with this book. You might read this book from cover to cover. You might only dip into the chapters that resonate for you. You might even start from the back and work in. Who knows? How you read it is up to you. Whether you use it in your daily life is also your choice.

But maybe, just maybe, this book will spark new conversations, new ideas, new relationships. A new You. Because working at relationships is not just an end in itself, it is a means to a better life and an improved version of you.

CHAPTER 1
Ourselves

Our relationship with our own Self lasts an entire lifetime. It has the potential to be the most rewarding relationship we ever experience, and it can generate feelings of utter fulfilment and contentment.

Whatever your circumstances, the one individual guaranteed to accompany you through the highs and lows, the joy and the pain, is You.

Yet too many people are crippled by low self-esteem or a lack of self-respect, which compromises both mood and behaviour. If, on some level, life is an ongoing quest to live authentically, we need to take responsibility for ourselves and the choices we make. And yet to make good and healthy choices for ourselves, we have to know and love ourselves a bit better.

But it's more than that. It's about developing the skills to feel content with what happens to us, with how we look, with our prospects, our careers, our other relationships, our life trajectory. It's about learning to love ourselves, even when things don't go to plan, when we make mistakes (which we all do) or when we feel hurt or inadequate. Above all, it's about feeling comfortable in our own skin.

It's also about recognizing that, as adults, no-one is responsible for us, our lives, and our feelings, apart from us. It's about recognizing that sometimes we search for someone or something (alcohol, food, gambling, porn) to fill the void in our own lives, a void we can fill differently by emotionally nourishing ourselves. In the end, *we are responsible for our own happiness, and for our capacity to love and be loved.*

Who am I?

Our relationships are a subtle balance of dependence and independence, but we must develop sufficient inner strength (we often refer to this as Ego strength) so that we can live and function and feel fulfilled on our own. To stand – and more importantly, perhaps, to *know* in our heart that we're capable of standing – on our own two feet.

However, we're not born knowing how to be emotionally self-sufficient.

Jules's letter

I've been dating since I was fourteen. I'm good at fitting in with the interests of boyfriends, but I have little idea of what I like. I usually have someone lined up before the existing relationship ends. However, I've just turned thirty and I want some time on my own, to see who I really am. Maybe even save up and travel. The problem is, I've just started seeing someone and the idea of ending it with him makes me feel ill. I'm really stressed by it all and I don't know which way to turn.

Regards, Jules

Jules is scared for two reasons, scared to take that leap into the unknown and live on her own for a while, and yet also scared that if she doesn't make that leap soon, any momentum will evaporate. She could then spend the rest of her life wondering who she really is.

Jules recognizes that she first started dating at school at the same time that her parents' marriage was going through a rocky patch. Even though her parents made it through the turmoil, Jules initially turned to external relationships to provide feelings of security. Having continued the pattern without a break, she has no sense of her Self as an individual. As a result, she doesn't know whether she can 'survive' on her own. Preferring to adopt what her boyfriends like, such as their music or food preferences, shows she's less confident about being able to achieve her goal (staying in a relationship, feeling secure) by standing up for her likes and dislikes. Her need to be in a relationship trumps her need to assert what it means to be Jules.

In Jules's case, we explore her history of consecutive relationships and her fears of being alone. To understand where such feelings come from, we look at her past. Intense responses to present-day situations often indicate that we're dealing with unresolved issues from our past. For example, it could be an incident or a relationship from childhood which has led Jules to believe she can't 'survive' on her own. It's also possible that the consecutive relationships of her teens and twenties were her unconscious way of inoculating herself against feeling unsafe or unloved. Yet today this defence mechanism has run out of steam.

Jules also works on strengthening her sense of self, which includes drawing up a list of her likes and dislikes, and asserting herself in what she wants to do socially. At first this unsettles friends and family, who are used to Jules being compliant and falling in with their plans. When Jules announces that actually she doesn't like Chinese food and would prefer a curry, it comes as a shock to some to discover that she is no longer a pushover. Over time, Jules recognizes who in her life is prepared to take her preferences into account, and who is not.

As part of focusing on her Self, Jules decides to study for an extra qualification, in copy-editing. For this she needs to attend a once-a-week class and also has homework, so her free time starts to be filled with Jules-centric activity. As a result of the qualification, at work she's invited to attend a conference in Johannesburg. Once there, she meets an editor who asks her to come and work on her magazine for six months. A thrilling new door has opened.

The career opportunity provides Jules with a structure and support underpinning her desire to find out who she is when not in a relationship. Through pushing herself, asserting herself, and enriching her skills, Jules discovers new things about herself. She can own the fact that she doesn't really like Chinese food, that she loves dogs, and that she wants to travel. She quite liked studying for the copy-editing diploma, but she doesn't want to do any more for now. She has ended things with 'the sweet boy' (they are still friends) and is not in a new relationship. Instead, she is enjoying feeling the new emotions singledom brings.

Afraid to be alone

If we panic about the idea of leaving the person we adore (our 'love object'), this isn't about our love for that person, so much as what they represent. This person acts as a refuge from our fear of being alone or lonely, and unless we know ourselves to be strong and to have support, sometimes we can't imagine being able to survive without this other person.

This feeling is a legacy from the days when we truly couldn't survive without other people feeding us and taking care of all our needs. We felt fused with such people, our childhood caregivers, and of course at one time we were literally physically joined to another person, in their womb. As we grow up, we develop skills that enable us to separate healthily from our parents or caregivers, but we might also without realizing it enter into intimate relationships to re-experience that security, that fusion.

Remaining single is no guarantee of wisdom and maturity. And being in healthy intimate relationships can actually help us grow for the better, as a person. Such relationships can make us more tolerant, more compassionate, more demonstrative, more loving, more tactful, more confident. They can make us less self-ish, less self-absorbed, less scared. Finding someone who shares our dreams, our values, our life plans makes us feel exquisitely understood.

But who are we when we're truly alone? This is one of the great questions in life. It takes courage to let go of the allure of fusion and feeling 'completed' and start to experience all the wonderful things we can achieve when alone. There are so many answers to that question, and the answer can change as we age.

Finding out who you really are

If Jules's story resonates for you and you find yourself sliding from one relationship to the next, explore your own history to see whether you're scared to be alone. Examining your past relationships and moments in childhood can provide insight into whether you've developed ways to prevent yourself feeling hurt or lonely or insecure.

Give yourself permission to really 'feel' or get in touch with your feelings. When you look into your past, you might experience powerful feelings, especially if you go back to moments that were painful. Instead of avoiding your emotions, sit with them patiently to experience that they're survivable, and that they do fade with time.

Also, write a list of your interests and dislikes. Add a list of things you'd like to do but haven't got around to doing. Maybe decorate this list with pictures of the objects or of places you want to visit. These ideas reflect part of your identity.

Top Tip
Practise standing up for your identity by saying out loud things like, 'I like purple' or 'I prefer fish and chips' or 'I want to go to America'. The next time someone wants to do something you don't want to do, suggest an alternative ('Thanks, but I'd prefer to see a Daniel Craig movie'). This way you'll start to define yourself in relation to others.

Having compassion for ourselves

One key component to becoming and remaining fulfilled is to be gentle on ourselves and learn to love ourselves. Having high standards can bring great accomplishments and rewards and satisfaction in life, but they can also lead to immense frustration. Too many of us have a tendency to beat ourselves up when we don't attain such great heights.

Yet the difference between regret and acceptance, frustration and equanimity isn't about being born a 'glass half-full' person. It isn't even about a preference for taking risks or avoiding failure. The difference lies in how we react to disappointments. Improving our relationship with our Self includes developing compassion for the people we have been, our younger selves who contributed to getting us to where we are now.

Charlotte's letter

When I was nineteen I got drunk at a party, had sex with a friend and got pregnant. As I wasn't in a proper relationship with him, and was also about to go off to university, I had an abortion. I'm now in my early forties and single – although not by choice. In my last relationship, which ended recently, I endured two miscarriages, and now all

I keep thinking about is the baby I aborted. I'm not sure I'm up for adopting on my own and I don't want to scare off future husbands by talking endlessly about babies, but how can I let go of my guilt? I don't think it's a religious thing, it's that I believe my lack of success in having a baby now is a punishment for that abortion years ago. I don't know what to do.

Regards, Charlotte

Charlotte's pain is clearly understandable, yet in addition to the trauma of the miscarriages and perhaps also the emotions surfacing around the end of the recent relationship, she's adding to her pain by torturing herself with the idea that the miscarriages are a punishment. This shows that she's using her guilt about an episode from her youth to judge harshly the woman she is now.

Charlotte has focused on only one side of the abortion – that it was maybe her one opportunity to have a child. Looking back, if she was able to have her time again, she wouldn't have the abortion. But we can't change the past. What we can change is our thoughts and feelings about our past, so that it begins to hurt or haunt us less.

Hindsight is *spectacularly* unhelpful. It completely ignores the fact that nineteen-year-old Charlotte was in a very different place back then, with very different needs and priorities. Back then, she didn't believe she was mature enough to give a baby the necessary focus or stability. These are rational reasons for making the choice that she made. There will have been emotional reasons too, lost perhaps in the mists of time, such as fear or anxiety, confusion or helplessness.

This is where forty-one-year-old Charlotte can have compassion for the person she is now, which incorporates the nineteen-year-old Self. The sadness at not having had a baby yet still remains, the longing continues, but the forgiveness can begin and the self-torture can start to weaken. It's not about pretending we can change the past, it's about accepting who we are, who we once were, and what we're feeling right now.

Why compassion matters

Developing compassion for yourself is a vital life skill and I urge everyone, no matter at what stage you are in life, to develop it. Life cannot be lived on a permanent upward trajectory and all of us will, at some time in our lives, have to deal with the knocks of life, or with things we wish we'd said or done differently.

It is how we deal with these moments that determines whether we're positively or negatively affected by events. Regret, for example, is a corrosive emotion. It can make us depressed or lethargic, and sap our confidence. It can also poison present joy. If we were as horrid or uncompromising to others as we can be to ourselves, we would be given a stern talking to and advised to mend our ways. *If we harangued someone in Sainsbury's the way we mentally harangue ourselves, we'd be escorted off the premises.*

Research has shown that compassion for the self greatly enhances one's wellbeing, and reduces anxiety and depression. It can even help us stick to diets or exercise regimes. In addition to these benefits, developing compassion for ourselves will also assist us in our relationships with others, as we develop compassion for both their and our own human frailties.

One of the keys to developing compassion is to place yourself in context – to try to remember as accurately as possible why you made the decisions you did, when you did. It might be, for example, that you chose a career offering financial security over a career offering creative fulfilment. By examining yourself in context you're better able to acknowledge the person you were back then. It's not so much about hindsight, it's about acknowledging that on some level you were a different person then to the person you are now. As a result, you may have had completely different needs, different priorities.

To respect the Self, it's important to be truthful to ourselves. When we're hurting or angry or frustrated, we need to acknowledge this instead of burying the emotion – not least because it will leak out in other ways. We call this 'acting out'. When you have a bad day at work and come home and kick the cat, that's acting out. We're 'acting out' emotions we're scared to feel and face.

How to develop compassion

If you find yourself in a similar situation to Charlotte, and you regret a decision you made in your past, take yourself back in time to when you made that choice, and remind yourself of your reasons for making it, even if those reasons are no longer relevant. Make a mental note when you catch yourself beating yourself up over things done or not done, either now or from your past, and challenge this self-flagellation in your head by reminding yourself of the reasons that were relevant in the past. By doing this you can begin to be less hard on yourself, more compassionate, and you'll start to see your choices in a different light.

Top Tip

If you find yourself repeatedly stressed by emotions that seem to overwhelm you, try sitting patiently with these feelings to learn that, over time, they lose their intensity. This way you come to realize that you can survive your own emotions – that they do not have to be overwhelming.

Improving self-esteem

Healthy self-esteem is vital for a good relationship with oneself. Developing and maintaining good self-worth gives us a solid base from which to engage and interact with others. When we feel good about ourselves, it bothers us less that not everyone likes us, or that not everything in our lives is perfect. Delighting in the positives of our daily lives (our friendships, our accomplishments, or just hearing that evening blackbird singing outside – and I speak as someone living in noisy central London, where somehow the delight of birdsong seems even more of a triumph) is essential.

Looking for the positives may appear trite; it may even seem at times like an impossible task, especially when the 'present moment' is filled with grief or shock. But at some stage it can give us perspective and the opportunity to gain strength from seeing a scenario from a different angle.

Dan's letter

I've been ill for a few years, and had to give up not only my paid job but also my volunteering work as a sports coach to inner-city teenagers. The good news is that I've now been given the all clear, but because of the treatment I've been left physically weaker and have a scar that makes me self-conscious. I don't have the energy to go back to coaching, so I feel stuck and boring and ugly. I feel like I'm at a crossroads but there's no writing on any of the signs. Please help me.

Regards, Dan

Dan's situation shows how events can derail us. At the time of his illness, Dan behaved in a sensible way (retreat, focus on self-care). Now he's ready to start the new phase in his life. But who is he? Losing our employment or becoming ill, getting divorced, or having to give up the dream of being a footballer/dancer/racing-driver can alter how we see ourselves. This in turn can seriously affect our self-esteem. Often the work needed on our Self is about reclaiming or reshaping that part of us that was healthy, or married, or had different dreams.

For Dan, the medical procedures around his treatment not only cost him his job but also his confidence. Now that the treatment is over, he has more spare time but this only highlights his emptiness and lack of self-belief. We look at ways to reach out socially to existing friends who have stood by him, as a way to say thank you and symbolize the time to move on.

We also look at work options that might prove fulfilling and broaden his network of acquaintances. Dan worries that the gap on his CV will prove unattractive to future employers, so we draft the covering letter to emphasize the positives of the experience, not least the abilities to face terror head-on, and cope with emergencies. Some problems in our lives feel insurmountable but the journey is made more difficult if we stay locked in negative thinking.

Of course, if a future boss were to be so impressed by Dan's positive covering letter that he offered him a job, this would provide a huge boost to Dan's self-esteem. It would be a huge boost to anyone's self-esteem. But the ideal is for our self-esteem to come from within. Dan's scar isn't noticeable, but he's immensely conscious of it, and believes people will think him ugly. This is a projection onto others of what Dan thinks about himself. To dismantle our projections about what we imagine people think about us, we must consciously challenge the thought whenever we have it, by asking, for example, 'what does it matter what people think?'

Rebuilding your self-esteem

If Dan's story echoes your own and you've had knocks in life that have affected your self-esteem, make a list of *positive* words you'd use to describe yourself. Similarly, describe in writing things that have happened to you in a positive light rather than a negative one. By doing this, you'll reframe your own experience and re-write a very different theme for your own life. Watch out for your own 'inner critic' and challenge yourself every time you find yourself saying 'I'm not worth it'. Start to build up a list of the reasons why you *are* 'worth it'. These are all bricks in your 'supporting wall' of self-esteem.

Top Tip

If you're struggling with low self-esteem, make a conscious effort to challenge your negative thinking by replacing negative nouns and adjectives with positive ones. Give yourself praise and recognition when things do go well for you, or when you do something that makes you and or others feel good. This will stop you being imprisoned by old habits or patterns of thinking.

Challenging negative thinking

Proper nutrition and moderate exercise show that we respect and adore our bodies, that we love our Self. Women in particular can be hypercritical of their bodies. Yet none of us (I repeat, *none* of us) is perfect. All of us (yes, *all* of us) possess inner and outer beauty. To challenge negative thinking about how we look, it's vital to understand how much air-brushing and photo-shopping goes on nowadays, in magazines, on posters, or even into the apparently incredible images of our friends on Facebook.

But photo-shopping and air-brushing are not the real problem. The problem lies in believing the delusion that such images reflect the only shape we are allowed to be. That, and believing that being a certain size or sexiness means that you're a better person. Learn instead to see beauty in every square centimetre of yourself.

And anyone who insists that beauty and skincare are frivolous pastimes needs to check out a cancer charity called *Look Good Feel Better*. Working with make-up companies around the world, *Look Good Feel Better* runs workshops in hospitals to help those being treated for cancer to cope with the harsh effects on the skin of the treatment. The boost to self-esteem is phenomenal and inspiring. For example, Dan decided to buy some concealer to lightly cover his scar and immediately felt more out-going, less self-conscious.

Being kind to ourselves

Loving yourself is a life-long process, with very few quick fixes. Improving our self-esteem can take time. Having said that, I'm a passionate believer in the power of good skincare for men and women to lift the mood quickly. Skincare and cosmetics, for men and women, have hugely positive effects on the way we feel about ourselves, empowering us with an aura of confidence and lifting the spirits.

Not least because, although stress is a perfectly normal, healthy response to external events, the human body is not designed to be assaulted for too long by the stress hormones such as cortisol released by the body during stressful episodes. It takes its toll on our skin, our sleep patterns, our appetite, and our emotions. Even fertility can be negatively affected by too much stress.

Being kind to ourselves includes getting enough sleep, exercising in moderation, and taking a proper break for lunch. This doesn't have to be a full hour, though I'm not suggesting a hasty sandwich at the desk or the dashboard either. As a psychotherapist, I'm conscious that one clue to a decline in someone's mental health is poor self-care.

So it isn't just about developing compassion, it's about paying attention to ourselves and being kind. It's about making time to relax and having fun. Anything that nourishes our soul (identifying the star constellations in the night sky is another great free one) is worthwhile. They are reminders that life is for living, not enduring. There is not, in my view, enough kindness in the world, and we may as well start by being kind to those closest to us, including ourselves.

Our need for acceptance

We want to be part of the gang, and so we often conform when we don't mean to. At the same time, who we are when we're alone is never quite the same as who we are when we're with the boss, or our grandparents, or our mates, or even strangers. Different settings shape us.

Mikaela's letter

I'm getting married in four months but drawing up the guest list has made me want to call it all off. I've realized I keep my friends in separate boxes and am a very different person with some friends to others. At school I was laid-back and lippy in public, but in secret I studied hard and got into a university far from home where my friends all spoke differently. At work now I'm a bit of a chameleon, which has proved an unexpected asset as I'm asked to write speeches for senior people in the firm because I can mimic how different people talk. But what do I do at my wedding? I'm terrified everyone will see me as a fake. How can I change – and quickly!

Regards, Mikaela

Mikaela's fear of being thought fake is perhaps a projection, a sign of her insecurities. I'm struck by Mikaela's behaviour at school, which was to study *in secret* in order to fit in. Maybe a residue of guilt exists, that by studying secretly she was making an unspoken judgement about the people who didn't study, which she fears rebounding back onto her. Mikaela needs to acquire compassion for the choice she made back then and be proud of the efforts she put in to getting good grades.

She also needs to strengthen her core sense of self (what she believes in, what are her values) so she can be confident in the face of any received judgement. At the same time, she needs to recognize that she might simply be judging herself, not least because at work her ability to be a bit of a chameleon has been recognized as an asset, a talent.

It isn't therefore so much about how Mikaela can change but how she can become comfortable with who she is. Praising herself daily and expressing gratitude for what she's achieved will start to underpin her self-worth, not just because of her career achievements, but also because her people skills have led her to be surrounded by good friends from many different walks of life. *We all can benefit from developing a nuanced appreciation for our individual gifts and strengths.*

How to stop worrying what other people think of you

If Mikaela's story resonates, and you find you worry what people think of you, or you worry that they think you're fake, remember that we're imitative creatures and from birth we learn to function in the world by copying others. Over time, we modulate our behaviour to feel accepted by 'the group' and feel as though we belong. We all do it to some degree, as we're never entirely the same individual in the company of different people.

Top Tip

Be true to yourself and remember that we all act slightly differently in different settings. One way to remain true to yourself is to identify and list your core values, which are the essence of you, whatever the setting. Polish your self-worth by listing your daily accomplishments, no matter how small, and take pleasure in them too.

Mindfulness meditation

Mindfulness is an extraordinary process of paying calm attention to oneself and the world around us in the present moment through meditation. Most of us spend our time reflecting on the past or worrying about the future. Mindfulness is about accepting things as they are, including our emotions or mood in the moment. Mindfulness is terrific for improving concentration and sleep, regulating awkward emotions, and enhancing the relationship with the Self, as well as helping us become fully present and alert to our experiences and emotions at any given time.

Mindfulness creates the headspace to let go of the stress in our head from our thoughts about plans, people, judgements, and expectations. I was taught a type of mindfulness meditation that focuses on the breath. I find somewhere quiet, usually sitting in my office chair after lunch, and close my eyes. Once I feel ready, I focus on my normal breathing, paying attention to the in and out breaths, noticing the difference in temperature at my nostrils between in and out, and the various sensations in different parts of my body.

For me, the key to mindfulness is to develop compassion for those moments when the mind wanders – as it always does. Whether it's my To Do list or a snippet from a conversation or last night's dream, I simply acknowledge it with a mental nod, as though it were an acquaintance in the street, and then return to focusing on my breathing.

The brain is meant to be active and busy, so having thoughts during mindfulness isn't 'wrong'. We mustn't blame ourselves for having a brain. The key is simply to acknowledge the new thought and gently return to focusing on the breath.

Mindfulness in your day

You can do mindfulness meditation in the bath, on the bus, even in the supermarket queue if you're unfortunate enough to be standing in one that long. You can also do it as you eat. Have a mindful meal, at least once a week, preparing the food, taking small bites, remembering to chew properly, savouring the tastes and textures, and trying to stay silent for up to half the meal (which for me is the hardest bit!). It's not about the choice of food so much as the choice of *how* to eat. Families report improved enjoyment at mealtimes, and people with digestion problems report reduced bloating and discomfort, and less need to snack between meals. Instead of food being something that fills a hole or is grabbed without thought, how we eat becomes part of our self-nurture. By showing enhanced respect for the food you put into your body, you're showing enhanced respect for your Self.

Top Tip
Start practising mindfulness meditation by finding a quiet place at home or in your office and focusing on your breathing for ten minutes to start with. Take the mindfulness process slowly, building up your time gradually, and have compassion for when your mind wanders. Try having one mindful meal a week, respecting both your food and your body.

Self-respect

Self-respect and confidence go hand in hand. If we feel valuable or worthy, then we're less likely to tolerate being treated shabbily. Whether it's service in a store or restaurant, or how our partner treats us, if we have a sense that we're worth more, we'll do something about it.

The problem is, if we suffer from poor self-esteem *and* what self-esteem we have is being continuously eroded in our relationships, we might feel it impossible to stand up for ourselves.

Vicky's letter

My father left home when I was small and now I realize that in my relationships I'm drawn to men who treat me badly. Now my partner has hit me. Luckily we haven't had kids yet, and I have a good career, but around him I feel so useless that I've become useless, so I'm not sure I can pluck up the courage to leave. I still adore him, but maybe it isn't right that he has hit me.

Regards, Vicky

If you have experienced domestic violence in any way (because let's be clear here, this is what hitting a partner means), please ring the 24-hour freephone National Domestic Violence helpline on 0808 2000 247. All the staff are fully trained and can speak to you and support you in confidence.

Even if we start out life confident and full of self-worth, some relationships can brutally dismantle this and leave us feeling utterly crushed. As Vicky demonstrates, her successful career doesn't make her immune from a dysfunctional or violent relationship. However, the relationship has left her with such a distorted view of the world that she's become unsure as to whether it's right or not that her man has hit her.

Manipulative, controlling or violent men are more attractive to some women than others. Women with poor self-worth or poor self-respect, or who've had unstable family lives, are often drawn to them. Other women who speak of feeling attracted to such men hope on some level to be able to tame or fix them, while others are drawn to them because they possess qualities these women lack, making them feel, in a perverse way, complete.

For women like Vicky, not just the physical but also the psychological cost of remaining in such a relationship is high, as they lessen or subjugate themselves. *Such women need to feel listened to and not judged.* Walking out on such a partner is much, much harder than it sounds. Vicky is fortunate to have a good career providing a steady income, but many women are not so fortunate. They may not have much money, they may have children they're concerned about, or they may believe that their culture will view leaving a partner or a marriage as shameful.

Women and children in Vicky's situation need practical as well as emotional support. Often, such women need to reach a place of safety before the emotional issues can be tackled. The websites of charities such as Refuge and Women's Aid offer terrific advice and support for women in such a predicament.

Yet none of us must be complacent. All of us in embarking upon intimate relationships need to be alert for when our partner doesn't treat us with respect. Perhaps we did not witness a respectful relationship when we were growing up, or perhaps we're so desperate to be loved or affirmed that we're prepared to survive on the few, or warped, titbits of affection shown. And then when we get badly treated, it affirms our core belief about ourselves, that we're not worthy of anything better.

Developing an 'I'm worth it' strength

If Vicky's story resonates for you and you've experienced domestic violence or emotional/verbal abuse, you need to urgently create a support network for yourself, with people you can trust. This will stop you feeling isolated, which will also help you gain strength. Be prepared to leave someone who hurts you physically or emotionally and *challenge yourself in your head every time you want to blame or judge yourself*, or to tell yourself you're not worth it.

Learning to value yourself is a hugely vital life skill. When we feel and behave like a worm, people happily tread on us. When we feel confident and good about ourselves, we prefer good energy. We prefer to be surrounded by friends and lovers who value us equally highly, not people constantly trying to drag us down. Not all of us will find ourselves in Vicky's dreadful situation, but developing self-respect or maintaining healthy levels of self-worth is one of the most useful skills we can acquire.

Top Tip
Practise self-soothing behaviour by talking to yourself in a loving, respectful, and supportive way. And look after yourself physically in terms of eating properly and getting enough sleep, which will also improve your inner strength. An 'I'm not worth it' tendency must always be challenged.

Self-confidence

A lack of self-confidence can make us highly self-conscious and can mobilize existing anxieties. It can make us despair that we'll never achieve what we want, and often makes us blind to what we have achieved.

Connie's letter

Even though I'm successful at work, whenever I fill out one of those magazine questionnaires I'm described as an anxious person. I guess it's true because I always worry about what people think and even though I've been promoted annually and run my own business in my spare time, I think my problem is getting worse. I look at other people and they seem so confident, whereas I'm always desperately aiming for the next promotion, as though to prove something to myself. How can I stop feeling so anxious all the time?

Regards, Connie

Some people would view Connie as a successful career woman who has achieved many personal goals in and around the workplace. Yet she lacks confidence. The irony is that it's partly her anxiety that has given her the drive to achieve so much at work and to set up her own business running cake-baking workshops. Sadly, this side to her personality also spoils any pleasure she might derive from her achievements.

I suggest Connie lists all her achievements, not just at work, but in her personal life too. This is a technique we can all adopt, on a yearly, monthly or even daily basis. It's useful to be able to reflect each day on the good things because most days are a blend of good, bad, and indifferent moments – it's just that it's easy to forget or downplay the good bits. Listing them creates a visible tally of positives to look back over on those difficult days when our inner gremlin insists on chipping away at our confidence.

I also suggest that Connie thinks about where her drive to get ahead and achieve comes from. Confidence comes from many sources, and so does poor self-esteem. Pessimistic or over-critical parenting or schooling can leave us with a sense that we're only loved when we achieve or excel. Once Connie has some understanding – some insight – around where this spur comes from, she will be better able to make peace with that experience.

The other aspect to Connie's anxiety is that it's her impression that everyone else appears so confident. I ask Connie to imagine all the significant people (parents, friends, clients) in her life are gathering for a 360-degree appraisal of her, giving us their view. Using phrases they've actually used, it becomes clear that other people see Connie as extremely confident. They don't see the anxious Connie. She works hard not to let them see it. Connie realizes that the people she admires are probably similarly confident on the outside, while feeling different inside. Her focus needs to be on believing how terrific she is.

Time to feel confident

Sometimes what helps can best be summed up in the not terribly scientific phrase of 'Fake it 'til you make it'. Assuming a level of confidence you don't truly feel inside is hard to do when you believe the odds are stacked against you. In fact, at first it feels cringingly forced. And I appreciate that sometimes even getting out of bed can feel like climbing a mountain.

But here's a story: I was once waiting in the wings with another speaker to go on stage at a conference. The man is a straight-talking, highly successful businessman, who has turned companies around and who has been courted by world leaders as a result. 'I hate doing this sort of thing,' he whispered. 'Shareholder meetings, political briefings, even when I go back to speak at my old school, I sweat like a pig and dread going on stage.'

On stage, of course, his well-prepared performance was immaculate; he made a witty speech, and answered questions off-the-cuff. The audience became yet one more gathering of people inspired by his performance. Only I had been shown a glimpse of the deep anxieties inside.

The remarkable thing is that acting confidently can instil genuine feelings of confidence, while acting assertively can make other people take us more seriously. *It's an act of bravado with the potential to become a self-fulfilling prophecy.* And it's the one time when I advocate something which resembles a Quick Fix – because in truth, in terms of our life-long wellbeing, there are no real quick fixes. They're the equivalent of taking an aspirin for toothache. Taking the time to get to know ourselves well so we can make healthy choices for ourselves is the only answer.

If Connie's story echoes yours and you suffer anxiety mixed with low self-esteem, list the words you imagine other people in your life would use to describe you. What phrases would you wear as a keepsake around your neck, and what phrases would you like to improve? It's also helpful to explore your life history, which will help you to identify where your lack of confidence might originate from.

Top Tip

To increase your confidence, create a visible tally of your achievements on an annual, monthly or even daily basis. This way, you can read back through this list not only to remind yourself of your accomplishments, but to challenge any residual negative thinking. And at the same time, you will be reframing your life experience in a more positive light, which acts as a mental stepping stone to the next positive experience.

Procrastination

Lots of things can prevent us living the life we want, but procrastination is arguably one of the most serious because it amounts to self-sabotage.

Penny's letter

I always start the year with good intentions, about changing my job and starting an evening class. But by the time I've got home, made supper and checked emails I'm too tired. But then at the weekend it's the same story: I'm not even tired, but I can always find better things to do than tidy up my CV or research a new hobby. Will I ever change?

Regards, Penny

Procrastination is a wonky coping strategy which comes about because we're afraid or anxious about an outcome. We therefore regulate these emotions by putting obstacles in our way, or imagine that other more vital things (washing-up, Twitter) have got to be done first.

Procrastination is easy to laugh at, but it can hinder our career, our achievements, our pleasure. It can even cause us to be cavalier with our health. Not only does worrying about things we haven't done weaken our immune system with all the stress hormones flooding our body, health-related activities can also be de-railed by procrastination: booking a cervical smear or prostate test, making dental appointments, failing to get that holiday inoculation. Random choices that could affect our life.

Penny needs to understand herself better, to work out what the procrastination is masking. Is Penny afraid of failure, of not getting the job she goes for? Or is she anxious about success, of getting the new job and having to make changes in her life, or having to meet new expectations from new people?

Procrastination keeps us stuck in a bubble. The bubble can sometimes be annoying but at least it's a familiar bubble. And familiar feels safe. The alternative is a world of unknown outcomes, and human beings aren't very good at coping with the unknown.

The good news for Penny is that procrastination is a learned response, so we can un-learn it. I suggest Penny identifies what her form of procrastination is, so she can consciously catch herself doing it and make a conscious decision to stop. Like Penny, we need to *challenge the rules in our head*, such as 'I can't start drafting my CV until my desk is tidy'. And we need to acknowledge whether the tasks are realistic – that is, do we have any intention of doing them, ever, or are they 'impossible tasks'? 'Impossible tasks' are obstacles we create so as to avoid tackling other things.

Saying goodbye to 'The Procrastinator'

If you recognize Penny's procrastinating tendencies in yourself, remember that it's possible to challenge procrastination. Promising yourself a treat or reward is a great way to keep focused, and it introduces more positive energy into the process rather than beating yourself up for what you haven't done, or not done as perfectly as you might wish. Because another aspect of procrastinating is that it's often linked to perfectionism. We're either terrified our execution of the task won't meet our high standards, or we're terrified that if it does, we'll have to cope with the success or the emptiness afterwards.

I also advise getting more sleep and more exercise. This way you combat one of the most common procrastination delusions, which is to claim you're too tired to tackle certain tasks. So creating a good sleep regime is a natural way of supporting the other changes you make to challenge the pattern of procrastination.

Top Tip
Become more aware of your behaviour and what you do during the day, so you can catch yourself in the moment of trying to procrastinate. At this point you can ask yourself, 'what is it I'm afraid of: failure, success or imperfection?'

Life-long learning

The journey of improved self-worth and self-generated pleasure can – I want to say must, please let me say must – continue as long as we do. By adapting to our own individual constraints, we can flourish and find new stimulation. And because we make new neural connections in our brain throughout our lives, we're never too old to meet new people, try something new, take up a hobby or follow a new passion.

Margaret's letter

I'm seventy-six and my lovely grandchildren are past the age of needing to be babysat. My husband sadly died two years ago and I now feel ready to move on and do something new. I adore gardening and recently I met the governor of the local high security prison. He suggested I come and teach gardening and horticulture to the inmates. The problem is, some of my friends and in particular my daughter are outspokenly horrified. They all assume I'm going to be attacked. How can I make them see I have lots of knowledge I want to share and that I'm not ready to be pensioned off just yet?

Regards, Margaret

Why do we insist on putting people in boxes? It's as though we're afraid of difference, or dread comparing ourselves to someone and finding ourselves wanting. Margaret wants to indulge her passion for plants and at the same time has been offered an exciting opportunity, as she sees it, to 'give something back'. Although she's never trained as a teacher or mentor, she knows she has great knowledge to impart and also experience, not just about plants, but about things like nurture, growth, and patience.

It's hard standing our ground in the face of opposition – especially if that opposition comes from loved ones. But again, knowing ourselves well can stand us in good stead. If we develop a gut feeling that this is what we want to do, we can explain it to ourselves, which can make it easier subsequently to persuade others.

Margaret believes that it's good to face new challenges, to stay mentally and physically active. And she convinces her daughter that it will be a good thing for the grandchildren to see her as an active septuagenarian. With all of us living longer, it could be an inspiration for them to see granny doing something useful and exciting in her old(er) age.

In this situation, it's appropriate to listen to her daughter's fears, but also to have reassuring responses. Margaret speaks to the prison governor to find out exactly what security measures will be in place while she conducts her training of the inmates, which she then relays back to her daughter. She also promises to keep her mobile phone switched on. This makes her and her daughter giggle, about how the roles are now reversed, from the days when Margaret and her husband tried keeping track of where their daughter was during adolescence.

To make good choices for ourselves we need to know ourselves well. What Margaret knows is that she is the kind of person who is reinvigorated by new challenges.

Living the life you want

If Margaret's story is similar to yours, and you want more out of life, whatever your age, stand in front of the bathroom mirror and argue your case for embarking on something new. This will act as good practice for convincing other people. Examine how different your life would be if you had complete permission and the money and the health to do anything you wanted. How different would your life feel? Now give yourself that permission to research that task or idea.

Top Tip

Be true to yourself. Identify your values and your dreams, no matter your age, and start ticking off a few more things on your own Life To Do List. Remind yourself that we only have one life, and that this is yours. What, when lying on your deathbed, will you wish you'd got around to doing?

How to live, not just exist

The cornerstone of your relationship with the Self is loving yourself. As you go through life working out who you are, you must also remember how unique and wonderful you are. This isn't about being complacent or egotistical or narcissistic. It's about valuing yourself. No-one has your unique blend of experiences. No-one has your particular strengths, nor do they have to deal with your particular weaknesses. Trying to get this 'living' thing right is less about searching for yourself, and more about enjoying the journey of being of you.

You don't have to wait until the age of retirement to try something radical or new. I don't regard myself as particularly religious, but when Lent comes round each year I borrow an idea from a (very religious) friend of mine who *takes up* something instead of the more traditional version, which is to *give up* something.

Frankly it doesn't matter what you choose to do, it's the doing that counts. Try reading a different newspaper one day a week, learn a few phrases in a new language, or take a new route to work. Habit promotes inertia and low energy. Change means we seize our own future. It takes courage to accept that we need to change or do things differently. But in the end, all that matters is that we challenge ourselves to live this one life we've got more fully, to the best of our abilities.

This can also include being idle and chilling out. Beware 'the busy trap', constantly being busy as a refuge from what we fear is a void or nothingness, but which could instead be gentle space for reflection or recharging.

I leave the final word to a woman I've never met, but who over the years has clocked up more than her fair share of comments about her behaviour, her looks, her choices. A woman who married into the royal family and had two beautiful daughters, but who then made some unfortunate choices and has been somewhat sidelined. In an interview I once saw, she mentioned some advice she gave her daughters when they were younger: *enter every room with a smile.*

I don't know what it is about that simple phrase that makes me well up, but it seems to me to be the best advice, the best free gift anyone could give another person. To prepare them for the way the world so often gives back to us what we give out. If you scowl or complain or retreat, the world will too. But if you smile, you stand a better chance of receiving a smile in return.

This is the kind of gift we have permission to give ourselves. This, and the ongoing PEP talk of Pleasure, Encouragement, and Praise. To develop our emotional resilience, we need to be as encouraging to ourselves as we would be to our very best friend, our favourite relative, or our inner child. This way, you can become your own life coach, or the cheerleader for your very own team.

If you pay attention to your boundaries, treat yourself with compassion and respect, and remain true to yourself and your values while retaining the flexibility required to be in a relationship with others, you're not only taking responsibility for your life, you're creating a loving, respectful attitude in which to engage fully in other relationships.

CHAPTER 2
Parents

'Happy Families' is an alluring ideal, observed regularly in films and commercials, but it rarely exists. It's a myth, rooted in ideas around security and unconditional love and altruistic parenting, and it creates multiple expectations on all sides. Because our parents are only human, their parenting will always be flawed in some way.

In turn, we can only parent to the best of our abilities, and we all have blind spots from our life experiences that affect those abilities.

Early templates

Our relationships with our parents provide the earliest templates we have for our later relationships. We're not always conscious of this, but the way our parents behave, and cope (or not) with life, and get on (or not) with their own partners and family act as examples for us in how (or not) to do it. Generally, we take this template with us into our intimate relationships (I say much more about this in Chapter 4, 'Significant Others'). We do this at first without realizing it, but over time there may be clues that make sense of the choices we make – and keep on making. If you talk about 'always picking the wrong man', it's a good plan to scope out your early relationship templates – with a view to gaining insight, not apportioning blame.

Hilary's letter

My father was in the army and we have a warm if formal relationship. But recently, my husband left me for another woman and I've started to feel rage towards my father. My son and daughter believe it's because I was sent away to so many different schools because of my father's career. I feel dreadful for this, as the poor man is now nearly ninety. I don't think I blame him at all, so why do I feel so angry towards him?

Regards, Hilary

What Hilary's story illustrates is that blaming our parents for our lives and what happens to us misses the point. Understanding our relationship with our parents and seeing how these have influenced us, that's the goal. And in Hilary's case, she sees she's always chosen 'authoritative' men – men who like to be in control, men who like order and routine and discipline. Not all of Hilary's boyfriends were in the forces like her father, but they have all had similar personality traits.

Hilary's erratic schooling contributed over the years to her lack of social confidence. This is another reason why she's drawn to more socially confident men. By the time she left school at seventeen, Hilary had attended seven schools in three continents. Even now, she feels she has no close friends, only her son and daughter. The schooling choices made by her parents were typical for the time, but Hilary remembers being sad at school and angry with her parents for not allowing her to school in whichever country they were based. Not that she revealed this anger to them in person.

So, it's not Hilary's father's fault. But to understand Hilary's emotional response to her marriage and its breakdown – in other words, to understand her own life choices – her relationship with her father is somewhere in the mix. What matters here is for Hilary to own her emotions, to have compassion for the young girl who felt she had to stifle the tears each night in her dorm, and who fantasized about seeing her parents stride into the school and take her away. Now that her husband has walked out on her, old emotions are resurfacing. She feels as abandoned as she did as a child.

This new insight about the past influencing the present means Hilary has a chance to process that buried emotion and to see how it has influenced the person she is today, without there being any need for blame. She doesn't even need to speak to her father about her anger if she doesn't want to. It's old anger, linked to her inner child. And because Hilary is a grown-up now, she can have compassion for her inner child at the same time as understanding and respecting the choices her parents made for her when they were the ones in charge.

How to stop being trapped by the past

If Hilary's story echoes your own, and you don't recollect much warmth from childhood, keep a diary of the strong emotions you experience in the present as a result of your interactions with people. Ask yourself whether they remind you of episodes from your past. If you're afraid you'll feel trapped by such emotions, *comfort your inner child: remind it that you're an adult now, with adult skills*, enabling you to choose new directions. As a result, you won't need to blame your past but you'll be able to see it in a new light, as an era that contributed to the You you are now.

Top Tip
To help yourself move on, acknowledge your own disappointments about your past. At the same time, understand that your parents did the best they could under the circumstances, even if their choices are most definitely not the ones you'd make today.

Separating healthily

One of the hardest things to do, in moving to a place of adult maturity in our relationships with our parents, is to step out of previously assumed child/parent roles. This is especially the case when our parents keep trying to pull us back there.

Charley's letter

I'm twenty-eight and an only child. For as long as I can remember, my parents have had tit-for-tat affairs, split up and then got back together. When I was fifteen, they renewed their wedding vows and, to no-one's great surprise, separated three months later. Two years ago they had another bust-up and when dad moved out I hoped this would be final. Now, they've both told me they want to give it one more try. I've begun to forge my own life with a good career and a flat of my own, but right now I'm drained by their chaos. How can I make them stop using me as their go-between?

Regards, Charley

As Charley is discovering, separating from our parents can be fraught at the best of times, for both parties. Yet separating from our parents is a natural, healthy, essential process.

Charley's parents demonstrate emotional immaturity. They've used Charley as a confidante and surrogate therapist for many years, without realizing how deeply inappropriate this is. It's an inversion of proper adult/child relationships, and blurs appropriate boundaries. This suggests her parents have a lack of respect for, or a lack of understanding about, the appropriate boundaries between adults and their own children.

The repeated break-ups followed by reconciliations, together with the showcase event of renewing the vows reveal a couple who can't function without conflict, without chaos. Some people need such drama in their lives to feel alive. Anything less dramatic feels deadly dull. Such people also often need bystanders or witnesses with whom they can dissect the drama. This 'feedback' is the way such people feel in contact with their emotions. Charley has been that unwitting bystander for years.

The good news is that Charley has a vision, to carve out some stability in her life. This gives her the drive to change things. This possible reconciliation her parents speak of is the moment she indentifies and acknowledges her own boundary: she is not prepared to be the bystander, the go-between any longer.

Such resolve requires healthy self-esteem, an inner support system so to speak. Charley needs to develop the self-worth to believe she has permission for such stability in her life. She also needs to develop the confidence both to communicate the new way of relating to her parents and to handle any conflict or threats of rejection that may arise as a result of Charley's new way of relating.

Instead of trying to get her parents ('The Other') to change, our focus is on Charley modelling for her parents the conduct she wishes they could adopt. When Charley tells them she no longer wants to be their go-between, she's aiming to enforce a boundary that has been significantly lacking in her parents' relationship with their daughter, not to flip-flop as they do.

I suggest she imagines this wish as a line in the sand, something she's not prepared to cross. She imagines the line as a strong yet warm purple, the colour she's just painted her new bedroom – a colour that seems to represent both her own identity and a safe space.

Charley also writes to her parents. In the letter, she expresses her love for them but also her refusal to be involved any longer in their decisions to stay together or not. In some sense, the letter is the easy bit. The difficult bit is to stick to this declaration in the face of any future anger or emotional blackmail from her parents.

We also look at how to act when they next raise the subject, as no doubt they will as they try to dismantle this alien concept, the boundary imposed by their daughter. Charley feels confident that she can say the subject is not up for discussion or change the subject. This might have to be done in a very explicit way, such as putting the phone down or leaving the room.

By setting and maintaining her own boundary, she's also doing her parents a favour by getting them to take responsibility for their own behaviour and choices. This change began when she acknowledged that she's no longer a child but is now an adult – an adult capable of making and enforcing choices. In this way, Charley can start to assume responsibility for her own life, her own contentment.

How to separate healthily from your parents

Separation from parents is natural and healthy, and follows a fairly predictable path. At first, we are literally attached to our mother via the umbilical cord. We experience intimacy with our mother and our extended family, and then we discover playmates at playgroup, nursery, and school. Then in adolescence we start forging our own identity in terms of interests and skills. We develop crushes on people or fall in love. Later, as adults, we can stand back and acknowledge our parents as adults too. Hopefully close harmony can prevail.

If Charley's story resonates for you and you're finding your parent overwhelming or suffocating or needy, practise being firm, by reminding yourself that you have permission to live your life not theirs. Identify the boundary you want to create with your parent, such as preserving weekends as 'me-time' or not being dragged into their decision-making process, and be alert for their attempts to dismantle it.

Top Tip

Give yourself permission to separate healthily from your parents and embrace the adult you by taking responsibility for your decisions around, for example, how available you are to them. Assert yourself pleasantly, which may include explaining that if certain unacceptable topics come up, you'll be putting the phone down/ leaving the room. This way, you'll shift an outdated pattern of childlike relating to your parents.

Parental favouritism

Understanding that our parents are as flawed as us is difficult, because we spend so much of our childhood believing them to be perfect, wise, capable, and responsible. The more grown-ups we meet, such as teachers or the parents of friends, the more we start to compare how our parents function in the world and start to find them wanting. One of the most common forms of resentment goes back to favouritism experienced in childhood.

Jessie's letter

All my life my parents have treated my younger sister and me differently. My sister was sent away to an expensive boarding school whereas I went to the local comprehensive. My sister is sporty and tidy like my parents, whereas I'm messy and overeat. Now I've discovered that my parents feel so guilty about treating us differently that they're leaving everything to me in their will. I'm terrified my sister will be furious, and blame me. Part of me wants to refuse the bequest, when it comes. How can I make my parents stop treating my sister and me differently, even now we're all adults?

Regards, Jessie

Parental favouritism is invidious and destructive. It's also almost the last taboo subject and not widely acknowledged – at least not by parents themselves. But children (as I explore further in Chapter 5, 'Siblings') are exquisitely alert for favouritism of any kind.

The less favoured child will feel diminished and empty; and it's interesting to note Jessie's overeating in this regard, perhaps compensating for missing out on attention or approval at home. The favoured child, on the other hand, may feel an inflated sense of superiority at being the 'golden child', yet also guilt for being 'chosen'. Whether you were adored or ignored, there will be pain or discomfort.

It's worth pointing out that some parental favouritism is intentional and appropriate. There's no point dragging all our kids to ballet or maths club or football practice if the talents of some of them lie elsewhere. And it's appropriate that older children receive perks for being so, such as later bedtimes or more pocket money. Usually in my clinical practice it's the child sent *away* to school who complains bitterly as an adult; that being sent away was experienced as a rejection, deprived of parental attention, physical affection, or the simple warmth of the family hearth. Jessie turned to food, as though her mother's cooking was the compensation for parental favouritism shown through expensive schooling.

Yet, now that Jessie's parents are 'acting out' their guilt by leaving everything to Jessie, she's uncomfortable. Her fear that her sister will be angry is perhaps a legacy of her own childhood anger at the favouritism, perhaps also a projection as to how she still feels. And her comment about rejecting the bequest reveals how uncomfortable she is, being 'the favoured one'. Rejecting the bequest might seem like an independent, I-don't-need-you type attitude, but actually the intensity of the gesture shows how angrily enmeshed Jessie still is with her parents. It's a defensive comment, revealing how much Jessie still feels the need to protect herself from her parents' misguided choices.

We work on boosting Jessie's self-esteem. This is so she can value herself and her talents and interests, and not turn to food as a comfort. As a result, Jessie throws herself more into her hobbies, which give her much fulfilment and which don't need parental involvement or approval.

Surviving parental favouritism

If Jessie's story sounds familiar, and you were not the favoured child, now is the time to acknowledge your own past hurts and disappointments regarding how you and your siblings were treated differently. Work out if there's a link between your emotions and moods and how you try to soothe yourself, such as overeating, drinking or taking drugs, shopping, or throwing yourself into inappropriate relationships. This way you'll be able to see if you've been trying to compensate for love or attention you didn't receive from your parents, but which you witnessed being given to a sibling.

Top Tip

Process your feelings of envy or helplessness towards your sibling by setting your own standards for fulfilment and recognizing your own talents. Remember, it's not their fault (or yours, for that matter) that they were favoured and you weren't.

Unresolved conflict

Many of our conflicts with our parents in the present stem from our disappointment that they're not the parents of our dreams. As kids, many of us fantasize that our *real* parents – nicer ones, who love us unconditionally and give in to our repeated demands for ice-cream – will one day come back to reclaim us. Or we fantasize about running away. One reason why novels such as *The Famous Five* and *Swallows and Amazons* remain popular is because they tap into childhood fantasies that we could survive quite happily without the horrid grown-ups.

Rebecca's letter

I've always had a difficult relationship with my mother who, even though she didn't work, was detached. But now I've had my own daughter Grace, the situation has worsened. This is because despite not being there for me, she's now all over Grace, showering her with gifts and attention. She also criticizes my parenting. I was admitted to hospital briefly for post-natal depression and now I worry I'm detaching from my daughter because I'm jealous of the attention she gets from my own mother. It's ridiculous! What can I do to shake this off and make sure I don't repeat the mistakes of the past?

Regards, Rebecca

Rebecca's situation shows how unresolved conflicts from the past can contaminate our relationships in the present. The arrival of Grace has triggered responses in both women, which have intensified rather than reduced the conflict. Many parents hope, without realizing it, that by becoming grandparents they've been given a golden opportunity to make amends for their failings as parents.

Rebecca has to do three things at the same time. She needs to nourish her relationship with Grace, she needs to honour her relationship with herself, and she needs to examine her relationship with her mother – in that order.

This is because, as I've stressed before, our difficulties in relationships will always say as much about *us* as they do about The Other. When we have the courage to work on ourselves, we gain in emotional strength so that often the difficult relationship either bothers us less, or our way of functioning in that relationship shifts. This second possibility often eliminates any need to go head-to-head with the person concerned.

So with the active support of Rebecca's husband, Rebecca concentrates on being what the psychoanalyst and paediatrician Donald Winnicott called the 'good enough mother'. This involves Rebecca caring for Grace physically and emotionally, keeping the toddler's environment predictable and safe, but also protecting Grace from those parts of Rebecca which feel envious, which see Grace as a rival for her mother's affections.

These envious parts of Rebecca we are able to process and weaken in the therapy room. To do this, Rebecca looks at her long-buried feelings towards her mother, especially her disappointment that her mother was not – and might not ever be – able to give more warmth, affirmation or positivity to Rebecca, even though she seems able to give it to Grace.

This is not to let her mother off the hook. It's about having compassion for herself that she did not receive warmth/affirmation/positivity from her mother, while also having compassion for her mother who is incapable or unwilling to love her unconditionally.

However, there's exquisite insight in the close of Rebecca's letter, around her desire not to see the mistakes of the past repeated. Just because certain behaviour has occurred in the past doesn't automatically mean it will occur in the present. Exploring how she has retreated from Grace leads Rebecca to wonder whether her own mother was a prisoner of her own upbringing. Maybe she was parented by a distant or unavailable mother, which led her to withdraw from Rebecca?

If that's the case, Rebecca feels she can empathize with her mother. Rebecca's maternal grandmother died before Rebecca was born, and she has never had a conversation with her mother about how she was parented. We often only think about having this kind of conversation with our parents when it's too late.

Focusing on the present – and letting the past go

If Rebecca's story sounds familiar, and your current situation is complicating an already fraught relationship, the main focus must be your relationship with your child or family. Focus on nurturing them, while protecting them from any of your negative impulses. Also, let go of your hope that your parent can be a different person. Otherwise, you're in Fairy Tale territory where the Fairy Godmother comes along with a magic wand and turns the bad instantaneously into good. The person we struggle with in a relationship may never change. They may be terrified to change, or incapable of change. Or downright stubborn, what a friend of mine calls Right-Fighters. They're always completely and totally right and we're always one hundred per cent in the wrong.

Top Tip
Mourn the loss of the parent who never was, the parent of your dreams. It's about deciding who you want in your life and giving yourself permission to choose. Also, nourish yourself, as though re-parenting yourself, by giving yourself encouragement, compassion, and reassurance, which will boost your self-worth.

Controlling parents

One choice some of us go on to make is who to marry. Notoriously, however, this choice doesn't always go down well with our parents.

Will's letter

I've always had a pleasant relationship with my mother and at first she seemed to like my girlfriend Lara. Then, when we moved in together, my mother started criticizing Lara to me in private, which I confess I told Lara about, which probably wasn't a good idea. Then when we got engaged, my mother started playing all sorts of games as if Lara no longer existed. Lara and I both assume it's because we've decided not to have kids whereas my mother longs to be a grandmother. Now we're married, I want to make sure the relationship with my mother gets better rather than worse. Please help!

Regards, Will

Will's mother and he differ in their opinion as to whether Lara is a 'good enough' wife. I'm deliberately borrowing from Donald Winnicott's phrase here, because just as no husband is perfect, no wife is perfect and nor is any marriage perfect.

The tone of the early part of Will's letter expresses his confusion. How did it all unravel? At first Lara is welcomed, but as soon as the relationship becomes more permanent, Will's mother changes tack. 'Playing games as if Lara didn't exist' while being nice to her face is what some would call two-faced. Clinically we call this 'acting out'. Will's mother can't acknowledge her frustration or anger that the relationship exists, so she 'acts out' the anger in other ways, by being difficult towards Lara.

Will suspects this situation is more than just the normal wobbles which occur in families when a moment of transition, a shuffling of the family cards, takes place. In this situation, there's an additional factor: Will and Lara's decision not to have kids. It's a choice that runs contrary to Will's mother's vision of her own future. And her predicament is likely to be replicated more in the future rather than less. Recent research[1] has shown that a third of female graduates born in 1970 will not have had children by 2015, roughly the end of their fertility years. For some women, this is a deep tragedy: full-term pregnancy eludes them, or the men in their life were never suitable Dad material. But for an increasing number of women, being child-free is a conscious choice.

So, Will's mother has lost control of the situation, of her family, of her future. Her 'acting out' isn't just about anger or frustration. It could be about very real existential pain.

However, her acting out runs the risk of causing real damage. With Lara being made to feel unwelcome, by trying to air-brush out one half of the couple, Will's mother runs the risk of alienating her son too.

Will and his mother must re-negotiate their relationship whereby Will is able to demonstrate that he's the master of his own life, his own choices. Will needs to 'dethrone' the mother in his mind, the mother critical of his choices, the mother he's been trying to please by keeping the relationship 'pleasant'. We see this in the way that, originally, Will told Lara about his mother's criticisms. Unable to stand up to his mother, he passed the information on to his then girlfriend, perhaps unconsciously hoping that Lara would pick the fight.

By developing his self-esteem, Will is eventually able to stand up to his mother when she tries to disinvite Lara from a family party. In this way, he shows his mother that he won't give in to unacceptable, childlike behaviour. As well as fully respecting his mother's disappointment at the lack of any grandchildren, he needs to *define himself in relation to his mother*, which includes standing up to his mother to show that marriage to Lara is his choice.

Talking of respect, Will's assertive stance demonstrates respect for his wife, which his mother can only learn from. Only when we show our parents that we cannot be controlled in the way we once were (for good reason) as children, will The Other then have the choice: to adapt and learn new ways of relating to us, or to lose the relationship altogether.

Healthy separation

If Will's story echoes yours, and your parent finds it difficult to accept your chosen partner, work on separating healthily from your parents, instead of having your partner cast as the villain. Continue to show love, but practise setting a boundary, with possible sanctions (such as not visiting) if your parent seems unwilling to change their behaviour. Boundary setting doesn't have to be confrontational. Instead, state clearly the point at issue ('X is my wife now, and I'd appreciate it if you'd treat her with respect') and respond consistently, carrying out the sanction, as you would to a truculent child, when the point is ignored.

Top Tip

You must recognize that your parents are not the idols you put on a pedestal in your childhood, and that you have permission to hold different opinions to theirs. This insight will help you feel more comfortable demonstrating that your loyalty is now to your spouse, not to your parents.

Fear of disapproval

From childhood we experience that being on the receiving end of disapproval can be uncomfortable. At the same time, as adults, we need to be clear about whether the disapproval is explicit or assumed, or even whether it's our own disapproval turned back on ourselves.

Bea's letter

I'm terrified to tell my elderly mother I'm gay. I was married for two long years, which was a disaster, and I was very miserable, although it was all my fault for being so dishonest as to marry the man in the first place. I've been leading a secret life ever since, which has been hard, but now I've met a wonderful woman. We've been together nearly three years and plan to have a civil partnership ceremony. I'd love my mother to be there but she's rather 'traditional' and I'm terrified she'll disown me. Please help; I don't want to lose my Mum but I do now want to be honest.

Regards, Bea

Bea would seem to have two sources for her anxiety that her mother will disown her. Not only is she apprehensive that being gay will be disapproved of, she still carries with her the guilt that her disastrous marriage was 'all' her fault.

First, this guilt-trip must be challenged. As I explore more fully in Chapter 4 ('Significant Others'), both parties contribute to a relationship. For every closet gay member of a couple, the other member will continue turning a blind eye or getting different needs met, enabling the relationship to continue.

Of course, Bea's mother may not react to the news that her daughter is gay in the way Bea expects. After all, not only will Bea be revealing that she's homosexual but also that she is now in a loving relationship. Having witnessed her daughter's unhappy marriage, perhaps having been deeply saddened by it, it's possible that the news that her daughter has finally found happiness might thrill Bea's mother to bits. Or at the very least, relieve her in that way parents often have, of wanting their children to be 'settled'.

Working with Bea's anxiety is vital, to acknowledge it and to prepare her fully for the conversation she wants to have with her mother. Sometimes with clients I do what is called 'Empty Chair' work, which, as it says on the tin, is where we get to talk to an empty chair. In this unpressurized way, we can practise saying out loud the thoughts, the beliefs, grievances or dreams that have been running through our head, sometimes for years. Meanwhile, the Chair won't interrupt or storm off or answer back.

Bea can't truly know how her mother will react. Even if people had 'form' in the past, they can often surprise us. Even so, Bea's work is about exploring the conflict (between wanting to come out as gay to her mother and wanting not to lose her mother), until the conflict ceases to be conflicted and there's a clear path ahead. There is, Bea is prepared to admit, a degree of selfishness here. She dearly wants her mother to be at her civil partnership ceremony, but also hopes that the conversation will be therapeutic. With a history of a sham marriage and deceit behind her, Bea wants there to be no more lies. This is what underpins her decision to speak to her mother: Bea wants to live more authentically.

Preparing for an awkward conversation

If Bea's story resonates for you, and you have things to say to your parent that you fear they may dislike or disapprove of, you might want to consider the Empty Chair process. It can be done at home, in a quiet space or room where you're unlikely to be interrupted or feel self-conscious. After all, you're only talking to a chair. Take responsibility for how you feel and what you want to say, and examine any conflicts from all angles so that eventually a clear path emerges. This will help you feel more confident.

I've even done a version of this on the rowing machine at the gym, muttering away to myself. The Empty Chair work allows you the freedom to experience what it feels like to say certain sentences out loud. It's like a rehearsal. If you were preparing for an audition or a crucial work presentation, you'd think nothing of practising it out loud.

Sometimes these sorts of conversations require a similar level of preparation. It can even be a helpful technique if the person we wish we could talk to is estranged from us, or dead. The key is that we're taking personal responsibility for our communication, owning what we want to say.

Top Tip
Understand that being true to yourself means that what you say may be welcomed, but that sometimes it may not. You can't control how The Other will react. What you can control is being true to your feelings.

Good communication

Living authentically doesn't have to arise from awkward moments, but it does remind us that good communication is the key to most relationship dilemmas.

Caryl's letter

I'm thirty-one. Last year my mum had cancer, which thankfully she survived, but it made me realize I don't have a relationship with my dad anymore. When I was young my mum said I was Daddy's Girl. I think she rather resented our closeness, and quite soon I think he and I started to pull away. I speak to my mum a lot and we share the same sense of humour and love of fashion, but with my dad I wouldn't know where to start. My friends say I'm seeing a problem where there isn't one, but I feel something is missing. Am I right to be concerned?

Regards, Caryl

It's not so much a question of right or wrong, although the phrasing of Caryl's comment does make it sound as though she's seeking permission to become closer to her dad. Perhaps because Caryl's mum once resented the closeness, Caryl may have told herself that father/daughter friendships are unacceptable or unachievable.

Caryl needs to take the initiative, to build a bridge to her father. Worried that she doesn't really know what he likes anymore, and convinced he won't be interested in her pastimes, Caryl is understandably hesitant. As a starting point, she needs to carve out some time alone with him, such as going for a casual walk one Sunday, and ask him questions about him and his life. Asking questions shows someone that we're interested in them, and that we want to get to know them a bit better.

The conversations are awkward at first, as both dad and daughter get used to being alone on these walks together. Each time they get back, Caryl is conscious that her mother is inquisitive to know what they talked about. Caryl says that at first she felt she was betraying the closeness she has with her mum, but over time she understands *there's enough love to go round for both parents.*

A shift occurs when, on one of their walks, Caryl mentions a problem at work where she must choose between her current well-paid job and a more exciting job offer but with less pay. Suddenly her dad starts telling her about some of his early career decisions. This then leads them to discuss some of the big issues we all face in life, which then leads on to discussing celebrities and politicians who seem to be making a hash of this. Before they know it, they're aching with laughter about characters in world events and soap operas.

'I'm so much more like him than I'd ever dared imagine,' says Caryl. 'He's even opened up to me a little about how he felt when mum was ill. He hadn't wanted to say anything at the time because he didn't want "his little girl" to know he was frightened. But once he got to know the grown-up me, or rather once I showed him the grown-up me, he was relieved to discover that I'm big enough to know he's vulnerable. I'm sooooo glad I went for that first walk.'

Building bridges

If Caryl's story sounds familiar, and you have a parent with whom you'd like a closer relationship, start building a bridge with them by asking questions and showing interest. Let go of any dream you may have that your parents must be perfect and remember that they're people, just like you, with frailties and vulnerabilities, even though your inner child would love them to remain strong and infallible.

Sometimes parents of the opposite sex worry they can't, as their kids get older, be intimate. That they can't share a hug because of society's increased hypersexual vigilance. We're in serious danger of losing appropriate intimacy in families. Therefore show affection to your parents, by saying certain words or giving them a hug. It may be unusual behaviour in your family, but by modelling for your family a different way of operating, you can have the intimacy you crave.

Top Tip
No matter how late in life you start, consciously demonstrate affection and warmth to your parents, such as posting the odd card or handwritten note, or giving them a kiss when you meet.

Self-sabotage

Even as grown-ups (some might say *especially* as grown-ups), standing on our own two feet can be a daunting prospect. Sometimes we sabotage it by playing the blame game, repeating patterns from the past and blaming our parents for things that happened back then as a way of staying stuck there.

Rina's letter

I'm thirty-seven, and the baby of the family. I've always lacked confidence and looking back, I blame my family for criticizing me constantly. My older siblings are all outgoing and even as children were capable of discussing big topics at mealtimes, whereas I always struggled at school with dyslexia and have never settled into a job. Even now, I feel I have to fight to be heard. How can I get my family to treat me differently?

Regards, Rina

It's always useful to look for patterns in our behaviour, to examine how we might be getting stuck in life. The debate rumbles on as to what most influences child development, whether it's nature or nurture or a mixture of the two. In other words, how much do parents matter? Recently, research has focused on peer influence, arguing that as kids we're influenced as much by our siblings and cousins and schoolmates as by our parents.

Yet we're hugely imitative creatures. Therefore, the fact that, on the whole, we spend our childhood being raised by one or more grown-ups means that we learn many of our life skills through copying or downloading what they do. If we have critical parents, for example, we can grow up to be self-critical.

I'm struck by Rina's use of the phrase 'baby of the family'. It sounds like a phrase left over from childhood. In the present, Rina is re-living battles from childhood about getting her needs met, such as being heard at Sunday lunch, or not being criticized. Re-living them gives her 'the excuse' not to get on with the rest of her life.

My challenge to Rina is to look at how much of her is hiding behind these old battles, these old grudges and labels. How different would life be if these fell away or if she stopped trying to receive positive family attention?

I suggest she ask herself why she still craves being heard at Sunday lunch by people she doesn't much like. Or to challenge herself as to whether there's an element of self-destruct in not finding 'the right job'. Challenging herself means rewriting the family script. This is a scary thing to do. It takes us into unfamiliar territory. If Rina gets a good job, she becomes visible – unable to hide. Sometimes the very thing we complain about not getting is the very thing we're terrified of getting.

How to avoid repeating patterns from the past

Anyone who has returned as an adult to the family fold for an event, like a wedding or Christmas, will know how easy it is to slip back into the old destructive patterns of relating within families, where conflicts or grudges puncture the idyll. If Rina's story sounds familiar and you're stuck with old grievances, the key to getting your family to treat you differently is to start behaving differently.

Benjamin Franklin once said that the definition of insanity was doing the same thing over and over and expecting different results. Also give yourself daily positive affirmation so that you no longer need to get it from others, which will help you believe that you have the power to change things.

Top Tip
Identify your goal in your family, then challenge yourself to 're-write the family script' about you by behaving, for example, in the exact opposite way your relatives will be expecting you to.

Together apart

Eventually, however, the tables start to turn and our parents become older and more vulnerable. They may end up relying on us completely, and not all of us are ready for that shift.

Susie's letter

Two years ago my father, who was a vicar, died after a long illness. My mother, as the vicar's wife, spent years being professionally 'nice' and in my view hasn't faced up to her negative emotions. Instead, she has become clingy and spiteful towards me. I'm thirty-nine and unmarried and although I feel horrendously guilty for saying this, I want to create some space between us, perhaps even find someone for me now. How can I separate without making her feel abandoned again?

Regards, Susie

All relationships are a delicate balance of union and individuation. I look at this balance more intensely in Chapter 4 ('Significant Others'), but the same applies to our relationships with our friends, siblings, and parents. If one side becomes too needy, too clingy, they're looking to the other person to contain or control their anxieties.

Susie's mother's emotional dysfunction is getting Susie down. She's also worried that it's stopping her getting her life on track. Unconsciously this could be a similar excuse to the one Rina used: blaming someone else for her single status. But the reality of Susie's belief must be acknowledged too. The time she spends with her clingy mother, and the negative emotions, are draining. Maybe now is the time for both women to reclaim their independence. Susie just happens to be the one to get restless with the status quo first.

The way to stop people intruding on our time is to make ourselves less available. First, I suggest that Susie carve out more 'me-time' for herself. This could include taking a refreshing holiday, taking on new responsibilities at work or taking up a hobby. This has the added effect of giving her the opportunity to meet new people, which could do wonders for her love life.

Yet this change in behaviour is bound to affect Susie's mother, as her only support structure changes. So Susie can give her mother a nudge in the independence direction too. She might want to suggest her mother sees someone professionally, to process the emotions not only around her husband's death, but also around the sacrifices she was forced to make to be a vicar's wife. However, this will need to be handled delicately. Her criticisms of Susie are the latest in a long line of responses showing how judgemental she has always been about 'feelings' and the people who show them.

As well as exploring therapeutic options, Susie could help her mother seek out local book clubs, social groups or even some voluntary work. Perhaps Susie's mother could acquire a pet – anything to start filling her mother's life with new things, new energy. These new activities, maybe new friends, would create healthy separation between mother and daughter. They would help take the pressure off Susie. And they would give Susie breathing space (or less of an excuse not) to focus on what she now wants in life.

Creating a more balanced relationship

If Susie's story echoes yours, and you're struggling with a parent who for one reason or another cannot stop using you as a crutch, identify your short-term and long-term goals, and then pro-actively aim for them. Perhaps write them down in a journal, so that you can't forget or postpone this plan to obtain a more fulfilling life, no matter how small the steps. At the same time, you might need to be conscious that your withdrawal, no matter how gradual, will leave your parent somewhat exposed, so nudge your parent to become independent by suggesting options.

Top Tip

Set *and keep* boundaries so you're less available to a draining parent. This can include identifying one day each weekend that is always your 'me-time', or setting a timer when you make or receive phone-calls from your parent.

When parents remarry

As our parents age, the dynamics in even the most settled, functional families can become disturbed. The passing years affect us all, reminding us (even if we don't realize it) of our mortality. This can add a complicating layer to parent/child relationships.

Hayley's letter

After a long illness, my mother died when my sister and I were in our early twenties. Within two years my father remarried. At first I was pleased he had a chance of happiness again, but my step-mother Mara is super-controlling. This came to a head a few years ago when she tried to disrupt my sister's wedding plans. I'm now in my early thirties with children of my own. I haven't seen our father for Christmas in five years because my invitations to come to us are rejected by Mara. How can I get my Dad to stand up to his second wife?

Regards, Hayley

Step-families are on the rise and can contribute to stresses between children and their birth parents. While I look at this issue in more depth in Chapter 5 ('Siblings') and Chapter 7 ('Children'), it's worth pointing out that many children – of all ages – can be thrown by the blending of two separate families into one new unit. For every patient I've had whose lives have been enhanced by a step-parent ('He means more to me than my own Dad. On my birthday, I took his name by deed poll') there are other families struggling to adjust to the brave new world.

Hayley is now married with daughters of her own, living at the opposite end of the country to her father, due to her husband's career. The new hybrid family arose out of sad circumstances (her mother's death), and now she feels she's also lost her dad. He's a successful businessman, and it upsets Hayley and her sister to think that in the past he fought fiercely for business deals but that today he doesn't seem to want to fight to see his children or grandchildren, or see them treated with more kindness by his second wife.

Even as adults, we want to feel the warmth of family. Coming to understand that our parents are fallible or imperfect is hard.

Hayley's father has shown he can be spineless emotionally. Mara is the domineering person in the relationship and her wishes prevail. When she refuses Hayley's invitations to spend Christmas with them, everyone loses.

In our work together, Hayley explores her pain at this second loss and the disappointment at her father's lack of support. We also role-play a possible conversation with her father, in which Hayley voices emotions that are possibly unpalatable to him.

But above all, the work is around processing the dismay and disorientation now that her father has fallen from the pedestal on which Hayley and her sister once placed him in their childhood. She and her sister also naturally support each other, and they have the love of their respective husbands and children. They can't change the fact that their mother died or that their father married Mara – nor can they change Mara. Yet they can begin to focus on the people who are there for them in their lives – which includes the warm memories of their mother – and work towards accepting Mara as she is.

Surviving parental remarriage

If Hayley's story echoes yours, and your parent's remarriage has complicated your relationship with them, take the time to acknowledge your own sadness and hurt. Find ways to soothe yourself such as taking exercise or a long bubble bath, which will show you that you're able to care for yourself, even though your parent is no longer so available. Understand that you can't change people; you can only change your attitude to those people.

Accepting doesn't have to mean embracing or even liking. It's about acknowledging that someone may never change. At the same time, give yourself permission to decide how much interaction to have with that person who can't or won't change. Remember, you have the right to put distance between you if they promote bad energy or act hurtfully towards you or your loved ones.

Top Tip
Mourn and then let go of the hope that your parent could have been a different person. At the same time, fill your life with people who give good energy instead of fretting about those who can't or won't give it.

Thanks for the memories

It's because the years of infanthood are so formative that our relationships with our parents can affect (some may say 'haunt') us well into adulthood. Unpicking our past experience to illuminate present behaviour is not only a classic therapeutic tool, but it has crossed into the global consciousness as a way to function or improve functioning. You don't have to see a therapist to examine your past. Instead, acknowledging the episodes that happened and especially acknowledging your feelings around what happened gives you crucial insight into how you live today and the changes you want to make.

But – and I speak as someone often found banging the drum in the media for talking therapy – there's a danger we can become stuck in the blame game instead of taking responsibility for our own lives, our own mistakes, our own future. Parents play an immensely significant role in our lives, but ironically we must beware of giving them too much power to influence the people we are today or want to become.

CHAPTER 3
Close Friends

The fantasy of a close friend is someone who is there for us when we're feeling low, enjoys our company, is able to celebrate our achievements, our triumphs, and yet who also lends a sympathetic ear when our world tips off balance. In an ideal world, a close friend knows everything about us and is still a reliable source of support. The idea that such friends have known us since childhood only adds to the seductive notion that we're capable of being known fully and yet still loved.

This explains why, when friendships go wrong, we can get so emotional, feel so bereft. We see a friend as someone who bears witness to our lives in a way that family members can't always do. And because, unlike our families, we can choose our friends, there remains the sense that friends are people we actively want to have in our lives. Therefore, to lose them can be devastating.

Feeling let down

The key to contentment in relationships is for us to be not so defined by one relationship. As a result, any ending doesn't have to be so devastating.

Nicola's letter

I don't earn much money, but recently my ideal job came up, for which I'm well qualified, and I applied. I happened to mention it to my best friend Cass and she said it sounded like a great job for her husband Colin. I didn't think anything of the comment, but three months later, Colin has got the job. I'm devastated, not just at losing out on the career prospects and income, but because I feel completely shafted by Cass. In the past, Cass and Colin have been extremely kind and generous to me, I socialize with them a lot and even sometimes house-sit for them, but this has left me feeling destroyed. What can I say?

Regards, Nicola

When we're upset, we often turn to great friends for support or advice, so it's doubly upsetting when our friends prove to be the trigger for our distress. Nicola's sense of feeling destroyed is because of this double blow, where the one person she might have reasonably turned to, to commiserate with over not getting the job, turns out to be partly responsible for her despair.

Nicola needs first to acknowledge her own feelings, a mixture of huge disappointment at not getting the job, and betrayal. She also feels cross with herself for telling Cass about the job, although Nicola could not have predicted what Cass would do with the information. Many of us place trust high up on the list of attributes of a good friend and we'd be appalled to think they'd take something we said in confidence and make it public.

In practical terms, Nicola and I look at the reality of the situation. There was no guarantee she'd get the job, although the job spec did play to her strengths. It's also important for Nicola to work on strengthening her own self-esteem. Missing out on the job will have dealt it a blow, but it's how we respond to life's setbacks that determines our mental health.

At the same time, Nicola's friendship with Cass has received a knock and it's possible that Cass is not aware of this. It's also possible that Cass is *extremely* aware of this, and may be feeling guilty. Either way, both women need to talk openly about what has happened. Nicola needs to own her disappointment, not that Colin got the job, but that Cass took Nicola's information and used it to her husband's advantage. It's a moment when Nicola is presented with evidence that, on some level, Cass's loyalty is (not surprisingly) to her husband before Nicola. And it's a stark dilemma many friendships face. How many of us, in Cass's shoes, would have done the same?

Friendships can survive such blows but honesty is needed to deal with what has happened. For example, if Nicola says only that she's thrilled for Colin, not only will she be denying her own truth, she'll carry her resentments without addressing them. Without realizing it, she may start to find everything Cass and Colin do annoying, or may start to get angry with them for no apparent reason. In fact, the reason will be the buried resentment.

The communication doesn't have to be confrontational; Nicola simply needs to state calmly her disappointment that Cass used her news about a job opportunity for her own ends. Most people would be extremely understanding of this, although Nicola needs to be alert for whether Cass feels guilt that makes her defensive.

This is also the moment for Nicola to decide whether she relies too much on just one friend. There is, for example, something faintly unsavoury about Cass 'poaching' Nicola's idea, after all the house-sitting that Nicola has done for the couple. Can Cass be said to have Nicola's best interests at heart?

Developing emotional resilience

The crucial thing is not whether other people have your best interests at heart, but do you have your own best interests at heart? Developing emotional resilience requires practice, but it means being better able to cope with disappointment. It's not so much about having tons of friends in case one of them upsets you, it's about developing a sufficient core emotional strength so that if people let you down or disappoint, your world doesn't crumble.

If Nicola's story echoes yours and a friend has let you down or behaved selfishly, own your own pain around disappointments.

Whenever you lose out on something, it's important to acknowledge the loss and the sadness around this. It doesn't change what has happened but it does mean you respect your own emotions and don't suppress them. Be as honest as you dare with your friend and be cautious of putting all your friendship eggs in one basket.

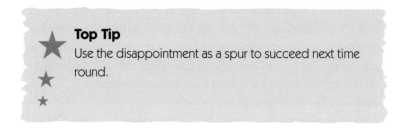

Top Tip
Use the disappointment as a spur to succeed next time round.

Toxic friends

Not all close friendships wobble because of an event or a specific rupture. Sometimes the problem creeps up on us unawares. A toxic friend is someone who either brings out the worst in us, or who exhausts us, mentally or physically.

Emma's letter

I've known Jo for twenty-five years, but it's a competitive relationship. If I want to meet her, the planning is such an ordeal (because Jo is always so terribly busy...), that I end up feeling desperate and needy. Eventually, when we do meet, the evening is always fun, and I love all our shared history. But afterwards Jo withdraws again, failing to return my calls, failing to deliver on promises made when we met up. She's extremely quick to let me know when my texts are too short, but recently I've needed her help and she has ignored me completely. Should I let her go?

Regards, Emma

Emma and Jo met at university, and it's been seductive to both women that they've been in each other's lives for so long. Each wears it like a badge of honour, as if having such a long-standing friend is a symbol of how much they're loved in spite of their failings, and therefore of how valuable they are as a person. Indeed, it's this badge of honour that has stopped either side calling time on a friendship that has passed its sell-by date.

It's taken Emma a long time to see that her friendship with Jo is toxic. A toxic friendship is one that brings out the worst rather than the best in us, or one where we feel regularly dragged down by an unattractive streak in the other person (as opposed to those periods in friendships where someone is having an off-day, or an actual crisis). With their put-downs or contempt, a toxic friend simmers with envy and hurt.

It reminds me of a client of mine called James. When James had his first article printed in a Sunday newspaper, his long-standing friend Angus could only say: 'Oh right. I never read that paper.' Assessing our friendships is about noticing when their energy has tipped off balance. We need to ask: *Is this friend building us up or pulling us down?*

Again, exploring a dysfunctional relationship will tell us as much about ourselves as about the other person. Emma begins to see that Jo's 'unavailability' is an echo of her mother's own ambivalent parenting. Emma's mother had post-natal depression. As an infant Emma learned she had to work hard to get appropriate maternal attention. As a result, Emma has been frustrated for years by Jo's style of taking rather than giving, but has endured it, trying to make herself worthy. Emma feels she must work hard at a relationship for it to have any meaning.

Sadly, when Emma suffers a crisis, she turns to Jo for support, but Jo turns her back. It's a crushing moment, but one in which Emma is able to see not only Jo but also her own behaviour in a more realistic light.

By letting Jo go, not only does Emma have more emotional energy available to deal with her crisis but, in the gaps where Jo used to be, Emma has more time to connect with the friends in her life where the relationship is more equitable, more give-and-take, more real, more rewarding. And she's now much more alert to the friend who can't be bothered. Emma has worked hard at valuing herself and now prefers to be friends with people who value her for who she is.

Having the courage to walk away

If Emma's story resonates for you and you have a friend who competes with you or who takes more than they ever give, ask yourself honestly whether this friendship brings out the best or the worst in you. Assess what you still gain by being friends with someone who brings bad energy into your life and whether this friendship is past its sell-by date.

Understand that we all find it hard to walk away from a close friend. Take the time to work at valuing yourself so that you can let go of friends who take you for granted or who can't treat you with respect. This will free up more of your emotional energy to be available to people who can be more than just fair-weather friends.

Top Tip
Hold on to the notion that a true friend isn't there just for the good times, but stands beside you during the bad times as well.

Loyalty tested

One feature most cherished in close friendships is loyalty. Such friendships can often break down when one or other side feels this loyalty has been tested.

Stephen's letter

Some months ago I was distraught to discover that my wife of four years has been having an affair. We've now agreed to separate. After a few weeks licking my wounds in private, I had a heart-to-heart with my close mate Mike. When I explained why I'd been out of contact lately because of the affair, I noticed Mike start to get uncomfortable. Then it all came out that he and a few of my other mates had suspected my wife's affair but had said nothing to me. Now I feel doubly betrayed, by my wife and by a friend who I thought would always be loyal. I don't know how to handle this, as I feel like I've lost everything.

Regards, Stephen

The problem with the concept of loyalty is that it means different things to different people. Some might think, as Stephen does, that it means warning your best friend when something is amiss. Others might focus on protecting their friend from pain, waiting until they are sure of the facts, or not getting involved in marital matters. Even the choice of words can reveal different perspectives: one person's help is another person's meddling.

Stephen and I look at this sense of betrayal and how it has left him feeling. He appears now to have become more upset about Mike's behaviour than that of his own wife. For Stephen, Mike's silence has been the icing on the cake. In fact, he's so furious with Mike that he's told him that if that's how he treats his mates, the friendship is over.

Stephen's relationship with Mike is now the collateral damage in the breakdown of his marriage. The marital collapse has left Stephen feeling impotent and ashamed. His wife is now living with the new man in a different town, and they now only speak through lawyers. She is, therefore, out of reach of Stephen's anger. However, Stephen has a new target to hurt. By being angry with Mike, and threatening to end the relationship, Stephen can, without realizing it, feel he has regained the power lost when his wife walked out. Stephen is angry about his wife, about the unknown rival, even about himself and how he might have contributed to the marriage breakdown. But all this anger is now being directed at Mike.

We look at whether Stephen's feelings towards Mike are justified. Stephen feels let down by a close friend because, in his view, if he'd been in Mike's shoes, loyalty to the brotherhood would have prompted him to speak out. The only way he's going to be able to explain this to Mike, and perhaps hear Mike's own view, is to *communicate*.

It takes Stephen several weeks to psyche himself up to make the call, but to his surprise Mike is keen to meet. Over a couple of beers, Stephen reveals how hurt he's been at what he sees as Mike's disloyalty. Mike is hurt too, because he hadn't meant to upset his friend. Instead, he'd tried to convince himself that news of the affair was incorrect. As a child, Mike's parents split up because Mike's mother believed mistakenly that Mike's father was being repeatedly unfaithful. Mike now realizes that rumours of marital discord in the present stir up uncomfortable memories from when he was a powerless child. He made a decision not to share the rumours with Stephen because he believed it wasn't his place to interfere.

Both men's separate life experiences clashed in a way that ran the risk of destroying their friendship. Stephen assumed loyalty would be a constant, whatever the circumstances; Mike, it turns out, agrees in theory, but finds that this one episode touched on something painful from his past. But by talking together, they reveal their vulnerabilities, which might bring them closer.

Sharing values

If Stephen's story sounds familiar, and you believe a friend has let you down, ask yourself whether you're taking out your emotion about someone else or a problem in your life on this friend. List the values that mean the most to you in a friendship and then discuss with your friend your respective values, to see where they overlap – and where not.

None of us bothers with setting ground rules for our friendships. It's only in playschool that we march up to people and say 'you're my friend'. Instead, we make our friendships up as we go along. By knowing what your internal codes and rules are, you can better assess whether your friend's codes and rules are compatible with yours – and whether it matters if they're not.

Top Tip
Try to have compassion for your friend who is as human and fallible as you, and try not to be affected emotionally when their values turn out to be different to yours.

The Pursuer vs. The Avoider

Close friendships often mimic family relationships. In many cases, we see more of our friends than we do of our real family. We go on holiday with them, we share memorable events, we seek their advice. Thus, not surprisingly, some of the dynamics that occur in family or marital relationships occur also in relationships between close friends, including the idea of The Pursuer and The Avoider.

Zoe's letter

I have two-year-old twins but three months ago my best friend Clare's first baby was stillborn. I've tried everything I can to help, but Clare just ignores me. I've bought her treats, such as vouchers for massages, and tried to visit, but she doesn't want to know. If I was grieving, I'd want my friends around me for support. I long to be a good friend to Clare, to let her know how sad I am for her, but nothing I do makes any difference. I did get a note from her recently saying she just wants to be left alone for a while, but I'm worried that when she eventually pulls through, she'll complain I wasn't there for her. How can I get her back?

Regards, Zoe

In this relationship, Zoe chases while Clare withdraws. The most likely reason for Clare's withdrawal is her desperate grief. Perhaps she's protecting herself for now by avoiding friends with children, as the pain is too great. And sadly, in Zoe's desperation to be seen to be a good friend, she's blind to what Clare might actually need right now, which is solace, empathy, and some privacy in which to heal.

As I've often said, problems in a relationship often tell us so much about ourselves. Zoe wants me to help her get Clare back. But instead, we explore why Zoe is so desperate for this. Zoe's need to have contact with Clare is based on her own dread of not being thought a good enough friend. That if she doesn't show on a daily basis that she's being a good friend, this makes her a bad person.

Zoe grew up with critical parents who made her feel she was never good enough. So in adult life she becomes The Pursuer while the object of her attention becomes The Avoider. I explore this further in Chapter 4 ('Significant Others'), but it's definitely worth highlighting here too.

The situation with Clare and Zoe is slightly different because the trigger for Clare's behaviour was her baby being stillborn. There's nothing to suggest that the girls' close friendship ran on Pursuer/Avoider lines before this tragedy. Yet for Zoe, separation from her dear friend makes her panic that she hasn't been 'good enough' and she cranks up her efforts to retain contact, even though such efforts run counter to what Clare wants. Zoe's panic is her own panic, but it's being dumped onto Clare – who already has enough to deal with.

Creating space within friendships

Healthy friendships work best when they exist in the spirit of unconditional acceptance. Often this means accepting that your friends are behaving differently to the way you would. If Zoe's story resonates for you and you feel you're the Pursuer, remember that you don't have to be physically present with someone for them to feel your friendship, warmth, and support. Remember that the more The Pursuer pursues, the more The Avoider avoids. If you keep this in mind, you won't put such a strain on your friendships.

Top Tip

Pull back the next time you find yourself chasing someone for an answer, a meeting or advice. Practise sitting and reviewing the feelings you experience when people don't always do what you want them to do, to understand that you can survive such emotions and therefore don't need to act on them.

Alternative visions

In an ideal world, our friends share our vision for how things are meant to be. Sometimes it's the fact that friends are not acting precisely the way we would that is a source of irritation.

Elise's letter

How can I stop my best friend Sarah trying to set me up? I've had a hard year with my mother dying and then I broke up with my boyfriend of four years. At the time, Sarah was great, keeping me strong. But now she keeps setting me up with men she knows (and even one she doesn't know!). It's got to the point where I don't even want to see her for coffee, in case there's some new bloke she wants to talk about. I've mentioned many times that I'm not interested in a relationship right now. So how can I get her to understand I want some time on my own?

Regards, Elise

Sarah and Elise's friendship is sufficiently strong that when Elise was having a dreadful time of loss and change, Sarah was extremely supportive. She made Elise feel heard and understood. And yet now, it's as though she's stopped listening properly. And this is a clue that maybe this current episode is more about Sarah and her needs.

Sarah is the kind of person who loves to feel useful. This is why she was the perfect friend for Elise during that awful time; her needs enabled her to give Elise exactly what she wanted, which was active support. But now the situation is different. Elise wants time on her own, perhaps time to properly grieve both the loss of her mother and the romantic relationship, and certainly some breathing space. Since much of Sarah's behaviour is about getting her own needs met, she is deaf to Elise's pleas.

Elise needs now to focus even more on herself, by surrounding herself with people who are there for her, not using her life to get their own needs met. At the same time, the only way Elise will be able to get her message across is to be firm and bounded. Not accepting so many of Sarah's well-meaning invitations will mean that Elise is also available to meet other people. This could lead to making new friends, which in itself will be a healthy development.

Creating more balanced relationships

If Elise and Sarah's story sounds familiar to you, take some time to identify whether you use your friends to get your needs met, such as to make you look clever or feel useful or to rebel against your family. This way you'll be able to see if the relationship is balanced or whether it's only ever about you.

If, on the other hand, you have a friend who won't listen to you, or is trying to orchestrate your life, try seeing them less for a short time. Actions often speak louder than words, so make other plans and generally be less available.

Top Tip
Nourish yourself with friends with whom your relationship is more equal and make yourself less available to people who try to control you or who want you to make all the decisions.

Group wreckers

Maintaining the group dynamic can be tricky because although we may change, the rest of the gang might not necessarily change in the same direction or at the same time or at the same pace.

Eleanor's letter

We're a gang of eight close friends from schooldays, who have managed to stay in touch well into our thirties. One of our friends, Harry, who was always stubborn, has become worse. If the rest of us want to go to a particular pub, he tries to change the plan so it's more convenient for him. We used to give in, but eventually we started being firm. When we do this, he pretends he doesn't know how to get there, or insists what we've chosen is strange or ridiculous. He also likes to claim he won't be able to come unless one of us drives him, and then when he's had enough of an evening he announces to the 'driver' that it's time to go. We've started meeting up without him, and talk about him all the time when he isn't there. What else can we do?

Regards, Eleanor

Group wreckers are people who (often without realizing it) believe they're not getting enough attention in a group, so they need to 'destroy' or undermine it. People who cause a scene when they arrive late for a college lecture or office meeting, instead of slipping in quietly, are group wreckers. It's attention-seeking behaviour. It can also be about a lack of personal boundaries, a sign of inner chaos.

Not all groups need to remain intact. But groups are highly alert for change, and group members usually (unconsciously) resist it. The group represents safety, so any change can be perceived as a threat to the existence of the group. It's easy to see, as in the case of Harry, when a member is ceasing to 'play by the rules'. The hard thing for Eleanor's group is to decide what to do about it.

For Harry's friends, the group has shrunk to exclude him. The new group has a new code that includes talking (or worrying or bitching) about Harry. Ironically, this means that despite his absence, he has become its unifying force. If he was to return fully to the group, it would have to change again, and it's unlikely it would revert to what it once was.

As a result, there may be an unspoken group desire to keep Harry out. After all, it's impressive that the core gang has lasted this long. Usually groups from school or college days start to splinter as colleagues or new partners creep onto the radar. Instead of fighting this behaviour, it may be time to let Harry go, as part of the natural metamorphosis of any group.

But let's suppose the group wants to re-integrate Harry back into the gang. This will require communication, and it needs to be handled delicately for it not to look like seven against one. Harry's behaviour suggests that he's resisting something. It's hard to tell whether it's the group itself and its social plans, or whether this is a broader resistance towards events or situations in his life, which are being taken out on the group. Groups can be like families. We often behave in them as we would to our parents or siblings, pushing at the boundaries to test how far we can go before they do the one thing we dread, which is reject us.

Someone in the gang, if they care enough about him, might be delegated to find out what might be wrong. Lending a sympathetic ear may be just what Harry needs. His attempts to change the social plans, and his demands to be driven to dinners and generally treated like 'the special one' may have its roots in something outside the group. Some people with narcissistic traits want to believe they're superior to others, and deserve to be treated differently to others in the group. They long to stand out.

Coping with group dynamics

When forming a group, we gravitate towards others who are like us, who share our interests or life experiences. Without realizing it, the group creates unwritten codes about what is acceptable in terms of clothes, sense of humour, or activities. Over time, these unwritten codes become tested by such things as work, marriage, or death. Some groups can withstand this degree of alteration whereas others cannot.

If Eleanor's story resonates for you, and there is a group member who behaves as if they're superior, recognize that this could be because deep down they feel exactly the opposite: insecure. Assess how you personally feel about the problem person in the group and ask yourself how you'd feel if the group continued, and how you'd feel if it broke up.

Top Tip
Delegate one person in the group to speak to the 'wrecker' to see if there's anything wrong outside the group or whether it's a problem within the group.

The Lap-dog

Rather like The Pursuer and The Avoider, there are other roles that people adopt in relationships, such as The Leader and The Lap-dog. The Leader is afraid not to be in control, and their motto can be summed up by 'I know best'. The Lap-dog, on the other hand, is afraid to be assertive, and their motto can be summed up by 'Anything for a quiet life'.

Alison's letter

I've been best friends with Kate for years, after meeting at work. When Kate got married I was her chief bridesmaid, but after that, we saw less of each other. Now she's divorced, I've been seeing a lot more of her. At first I was happy at this shift – she wanted to lean on me and cry on my shoulder. But now two years on, I feel drained by her life and its endless chaos. She decides when we meet and then spends the evening complaining about her ex-husband or the mutual friends of ours who have rejected her. She also has a three-year-old, and expects me to baby-sit so she can go dating. The problem is, she'll get angry if I say anything. How can I get her to change?

Regards, Alison

Alison's close friendship with Kate has altered over time, and not for the better. Through her loyalty to a friendship of some twelve years standing, Alison is now selling herself short. She's the cheap babysitter, the shoulder to cry on, but she is also now deeply frustrated.

As in many relationships, Alison's frustrations tell us as much about her as about the relationship itself. Her need to be needed has found a match with someone who has a complementary need: to be in control. We sometimes call such people The Leader, whereas Alison in this scenario is The Lap-dog.

Of course, for The Leader to be the one in control – and for this to occur over a period of time – the other party in the relationship needs to be, maybe without realizing it, content to play the more passive role of Lap-dog. There can't be two Leaders. And the way in which these two personality types dovetail together explains why such relationships limp along, often for years.

Ironically, what you often find in relationships like these is that both sides often also resent their roles. The Leader resents having to do all the work in the relationship, such as making the plans, while The Lap-dog resents that the other person is so bossy, so uncompromising, so controlling. People will complain repeatedly about a particular friendship, without doing anything concrete about it. What this usually means is that some unconscious need is being met, despite the frustrations. We call this the *secondary gain*, and it explains why some of us put up with or complain about certain aggravating situations for years on end. People who complain for years about their job act like this, as a way to avoid the more scary option of finding a new job and all the unknown scenarios this might generate, like new colleagues and new problems.

When friendships stagger on as Alison and Kate's has, it's because, despite annoyances, both sides are getting their unconscious needs met in unhealthy ways. Leaders get to feel safely in control, while Lap-dogs get to avoid confrontation or rejection.

Encouragingly, the healthy part of Alison is getting bored of the current dynamic. She doesn't want to be the punch-bag or the unpaid babysitter anymore. Instead, Alison joins a running group that meets twice a week. Not only will she be busy more frequently, but she'll also meet a new group of people with a shared interest. Out of this shift in her focus, Alison can see that babysitting for a friend is not itself a bad thing. In fact, it's a lovely gift to be able to offer once in a while. Being treated as a doormat is definitely to be avoided.

This is the kind of moment when I see people discover their inner motivation (irrespective of what advice they've received up to this point) to *conduct a Friendship Audit*.

The Friendship Audit

If Alison's story echoes your own, and a particular friendship is wearing you down, consider conducting a Friendship Audit. It's something we can all benefit from doing from time to time. It's when we reflect on our close friendships and assess whether they still give us fulfilment or pleasure. Is there a friend you always agree to meet, but somehow always cancel on the day? Someone whose phone calls you always divert to voicemail, or whose texts you never quite get round to answering? Or someone whose company leaves you feeling drained?

It's worth remembering that we can't expect to enjoy exactly the same things from all our friendships. Some people share our hobbies, know us from school, help us let off steam, challenge us intellectually, or bring out the very best in us. Some friends we might see once in a blue moon and pick up exactly where we left off last time, while others are in our lives every day and provide continuity. You may find that some of the things you used to get from a particular friendship – fun, mutual support – are no longer present. The friendship has become painfully unbalanced.

Having acquired insights about your friendship, you now have the opportunity to focus more on strengthening yourself and work out what you want out of a close friend. Another aspect of the audit process is that it enables you to see your part in any relationship breakdown or contribution to the current imbalance.

These insights will then pave the way for you to start to learn to respect yourself, which will help you set better boundaries for yourself in the future.

Top Tip

To receive respect in future relationships with friends, you have to learn to respect yourself. Being too available, too soft, can damage your friendship just as much as being too obstinate or too demanding.

It's also worth remembering that all relationships shift over time. We all go through bad patches, and true friendships may have to weather a few storms. Luckily, when they reach crisis point, there are a number of things we can do to put things back on an even keel.

How to put a friendship back on track

Ask yourself whether this is a friendship you actively want to save. To do this you'll need to be quite ruthless about your own psychology. Why are you still friends with this person? What do you get out of staying in touch? Do they make you feel needed? Do they make you feel important, superior, successful? Or are you always trying to be like them? Do you feel sorry for them? Do you take comfort from the fact that they feel sorry for you? Do they allow you to pretend that you're younger, more free, less lonely than you really are? Does this friendship drain you of energy?

Do you have the courage to stop being a doormat? Are you ready to stand up for yourself and your beliefs, and demonstrate that you're no longer going to be pushed around? After all, people can only walk all over us if we let them. Or is it time to back away and give your friend more space? Setting boundaries is important in all relationships, even friendships that go back decades.

Try to find out whether your friend feels the same way as you do about any difficulties. There is, after all, no point flogging a dead horse if your friend is already cantering away from you on another one. Is your friend aware you even have frustrations? Could you go for a coffee or a beer, like Stephen, to discuss things? Or have things gone too far, like Emma and Jo? Is any tension a temporary blip, a result of being too busy in a new job, for example, or is there something deeper and more specific about you and your friend.

If you do meet to discuss a relationship dilemma, resolve to listen patiently and not be judgemental. Try to understand your friend's point of view, and be alert for whether they're paying you the same respect. Perhaps declare at the outset that you'll both be trying to do this: to say, just because we're friends, doesn't mean we'll always share the same point of view. It may well be that by the end of the meeting you'll have to agree to disagree about certain aspects of a situation or history.

The final piece of advice is to reaffirm the friendship, if you decide to continue it. You could perhaps celebrate it concretely, raise a glass, shake hands, to mark it as a rubicon crossed. Perhaps arrange to do something specific together, to move on concretely from the previous log-jam. And in the future, avoid dwelling on what caused the initial breakdown.

How to cope with the end of a friendship

Sadly, some friendships do not last. Some wither away discretely. Others bow out in a blaze of glory, recrimination or hostility.

Others fester for years before dying by default. Happily, there are ways to cope with such sad times if they happen.

As I've mentioned before, friendships are vital to our sense of wellbeing, so the first thing to do when pining the ending of a once-valued relationship is to acknowledge the emotions this ending brings up. The feelings could range from hurt to disappointment, to anger, maybe even guilt that things didn't work out. And like all periods of mourning, the emotions can fade and then come back again before they disappear for good. Perhaps find a different person to talk to about such feelings, so that you can own the feelings and begin to process them. I promise you, the feelings will not always feel so fierce.

And as I cannot stress enough, when things go wrong in a relationship, it usually says as much about us as it does about the other person or the relationship itself. *There will always be something we can learn about ourselves as a result of a relationship ending* – uncomfortable as this may be. Alison learned that she had too high a desire to be needed, Stephen that he had not fully explored his anger and impotence around his marital breakdown, Emma that her need for affirmation, even from an unreliable source, made her too tolerant of a needy friend.

To forgive . . .

When a friendship ruptures, remember – forgiveness is an option. It's possible to forgive a friend who hurts you, or who withdraws in the belief you've hurt them. It's a big step, a very difficult step, and few of us are brave enough to risk it. Few of us feel strong enough to be the forgiving type. We worry that forgiveness looks like condoning shoddy behaviour. That it's a glib word, meaning little.

True forgiveness is subtly different. Forgiveness, not even in a religious sense, is something you give because you want to give it, not out of any ulterior motive as to what you might hope to receive in return. If authentically given, forgiveness can be a step towards personal peace and healing.

. . . or not to Forgive

Regrettably, not even forgiveness will rekindle all friendships. It's possible that some friendships are not meant to be, or have outlived their life. A friend of mine once advised me that some people will surprise you in a good way, and others will surprise you in a bad way. So sometimes it's about accepting the reality of that unfortunate truth.

As with all loss, coping with the brave new world after the demise of any relationship may involve a period of mourning the ending, before moving on. Moving on can be achieved by spending time with other existing friends, with family, or by joining new groups in order to make new friends. You may find a period of reflection helpful, perhaps rebuilding a bit of confidence, with solitary activities such as meditating or yoga to build mental or physical strength before launching yourself on the world again. Or you may want to take up a hobby (kick-boxing is a great, safe way for venting any anger or frustration). New hobbies occupy time, which prevents brooding and injects fresh energy into our lives.

Cicero said that 'Life is nothing without Friendship'. Close friends are vital to our mental wellbeing. They keep us grounded, understand us, and provide healthy emotional support. They love us for all our faults, so we don't need to focus on the air-brushed versions on Facebook or Twitter. The mistake comes in investing too much time in 'virtual' friends at the expense of the unique and precious wonderfulness of our real ones. Real close friendships can be the most illuminating, the most instructive of our lives.

CHAPTER 4
Significant Others

Intimate relationships are the very cornerstone of human social existence. They have the potency, the passion, to turn us giddy with delight, to make us feel ravished, adored, energized, confident, complete.

They also have the power, the fire, to destroy our equilibrium, our sanity, our self-worth, our very sense of self. And for some, the pain, the devastation of heartbreak alters our behaviour as dramatically as if we had been burned by fire. Why, we often ask, would we dare put ourselves through that again?

Yet as one of my letter writers below discovers, as she tries to work out how to *avoid* a broken heart, the price for this protective isolation is a guarantee of missing out on the beautiful life-enhancing things intimate relationships can bring, the warmth, the love, and the potential for growth.

Love isn't just something we 'fall' into. Long-lasting love, durable, fulfilling love takes a lot of work and self-awareness. An intimate relationship was once summed up for me by one of my clients as 'effort in, reward out'. The more we put in, the more we put ourselves on the line, the more rewarding our intimate relationships can be. However, this also explains why, when our intimate relationships go wrong, we often feel traumatized. Sometimes we can feel almost destroyed, so massive has been our investment in a particular relationship.

Echoes of the past

Understanding how we enter intimate relationships, what we bring to them from our past, and distinguishing fantasy from reality can help us know ourselves better.

Ed's letter

I'm forty-one and I don't trust women. When I was five my mother left me and my younger sister to live with her lover. I think for years I was angry at her for leaving, and angry at my sister for being someone I now had to take care of (my father was a lovely man, but a hopeless parent). Now, even though I'm married and have a wonderful son, I constantly need confirmation that a woman likes me or finds me attractive. I've had many affairs during my marriage but just recently my wife has told me she's in love with someone else and wants a divorce. I'm utterly devastated. What can I do to get my wife to love me again?

Regards, Ed

Ed is right to incorporate his childhood into this very sad tale of betrayal and unhappiness. Ed has betrayed his wife for years, not least because he's been angry with a different woman for even longer. Ed's mother's abandonment of her children for a lover when they were so young suggests that her maternal focus was at least partly elsewhere. This will have affected her mothering. Ed speaks of being lonely and angry when she left. Losing trust with anyone is hard but losing it within the family can be devastating. It shakes our sense of security. In Ed's case, it has contributed to his overwhelming need to know that women still like him or, as an adult, still fancy him or find him indispensible.

The anger, the loneliness, and the constant need for reassurance are understandable in a five-year-old. As an adult, the constant reassurance Ed seeks from women is inappropriate. It's a legacy of trying to fill a hole that is very clearly 'Ed's-mother' shape. Even the intimacy of marriage is not enough to fill the hole and soon Ed is off, having affairs because on some level he's still deeply affected by what happened to him as a child. These affairs are short-lived, or superficial, and end with Ed getting angry that his lovers aren't giving him the total attention or sense of being important he thinks he needs to survive. Ed behaves like an 'entitled child' in his adult relationships with women. And that's because what he wants is not an adult relationship (in which he can both grow and grow up), but to repair the damage of his childhood.

This fault-line in our intimate relationships is common. This is because in our intimate relationships we often look for someone who 'fits' and replicates that early template. Many of us long to get the love and affirmation we believe we missed out on as a child and we carry this longing with us into our adult relationships.

Other couples get together with less of an *obvious* 'fit' ('what on earth does she see in him?" or "he must be doing something she likes, nudge nudge"). But there's always a fit. And usually we're totally unaware of it. It's unconscious.

When Ed asks how to get his wife to love him again, he reveals how, for him, marriage is about getting his needs met. As far as Ed is concerned, this comes before addressing how *he* might need to change to have a chance of more healthy relations with women in the future.

Ed works on understanding that for decades he's been trying to get the women in his life to love him as completely and uncondi-tionally as he longed his mother to do. He and I also work on processing and managing his anger – one aspect of his adult relations with women that rapidly turns them off. This rejection of him is then a re-run of Ed losing his mother, which only stokes his deep reserves of anger.

We also explore Ed's relationship with his sister. As an adult Ed has often, without realizing it, had affairs with 'needy' women or women he imagines need rescuing. This repeats a pattern from his childhood when he believed he had to protect/raise/rescue his sister. Therefore, his anger is often directed at confident or unavailable women whose life situations prevent Ed from repeating the role of rescuer.

Healing early hurts

If Ed's story has resonated for you and you've had multiple affairs or you've identified a particular relationship breakdown pattern, identify what it is you're trying to repair from your past in your present relationships.

When two people enter deeply into a relationship, it's inevitable they'll trigger each other's deepest wounds and sore points. These wounds always have their origin in something that occurred 'early' in our lives. This shows that a proper connection is taking place. Each person in the couple will push the other's button, such as a fear of abandonment, intimacy, inconsistency or being unlovable.

But, at that moment of button-pressing, each person sees The Other as a monster who must be defended against. The Other is seen as selfish or hateful or abusive or deliberately cruel. It's The Other, we cry, who must change for this relationship to survive. It's a painful moment in relationships because it is proof The Other is separate to us, not a fused version of us. We can't bear that we cannot control The Other – that *we can only control ourselves.*

Your focus is not on getting The Other to change, it's to work on yourself. Assess what are your primary needs in a relationship, and what you expect to get from your partner. Also strike a balance between what you give and what you get in your intimate relationship.

Top Tip

Ask yourself whether you have unmet needs (for love, attention, freedom, compassion or respect) left over from childhood. This will help you to understand your own particular 'early hurt' (it will be different for each of us) and stop blaming The Other for not meeting that need. This will defuse a lot of unhealthy drama from your relationships.

Unrequited love

As a couple, trust grows when we start to accept and share our fears and vulnerabilities. Written on the page this sounds rather straightforward, but it's a very hard, very brave thing to do in a relationship. The reason why it's brave is because by entering into a relationship, we're entering into the unknown. We're taking a risk, a risk with our heart. We can't, for example, force people to love us back.

Beverly's letter

I've known Paul since university when we shared a flat with two others. We've been great friends for ten years and then last year on a trip to Cornwall we realized our feelings for each other were stronger and we started dating. However, last month he told me being my boyfriend doesn't feel right, so we've split up and I haven't seen him since. I'm completely devastated. I thought relationships based on friendship stood the best chance of success. How can I get him to see that we're so good together?

Regards, Beverly

Beverly's situation is complicated by the fact that not only has she lost a boyfriend, she's lost an old friend. Since the split, she hasn't seen Paul at all. In most cases of heartbreak, we turn to our close friends for support, guidance or comfort. Beverly has now lost one of her prime sources of support. All heartbreak is painful and distressing but it would not be an exaggeration to say that Beverly is grieving twice over.

Beverly, in the immediate pain of separation, longs for union once more. This will be a familiar pattern to those of us who have experienced heartbreak. It reveals how much we lose ourselves in relationships.

With Beverly we explore her feelings of loss and look at how this makes her feel about herself. Beverly believes she's made a mistake. She feels stupid for believing that relationships based on friendship always succeed. This is a mantra Beverly has 'downloaded' (we say introjected) from somewhere, maybe from magazines, maybe in childhood from her parents, or maybe from observing other relationships among her peer group or people in the public eye. Or it could be a 'code' she has, without realizing it, developed herself. Often these codes are designed to keep us safe, to stop us taking risks. And in a different relationship this code could prove accurate. Unfortunately, for the relationship with Paul, it didn't.

What Beverly sees is that there's no perfect formula for intimate relationships. A relationship that grows out of a proper friendship stands a pretty good chance. Yet as Harry and Sally discover in the eponymous movie, intimacy and sex add new dimensions to relationships, new joys but also new complications. Not all friendships can make the crossover into deeper intimacy.

Losing Paul has also left Beverly feeling worthless and unlovable. It's another reason why she wants him back, so that she can feel worthy and lovable again. It's a way to make us feel whole. Looked at in this way we see that the ideal is not to rely on The

Other to make us feel worthy and lovable. The ideal is for that feeling of worthiness and attractiveness to come from within. That way, it's always there, a home-grown supply of emotional nourishment. Part of becoming emotionally mature is developing resilience, and being able to stand on our own two feet. And it's hard to do. There's always a little part of us unwilling to let go of the inner child that longs to be held and comforted by others instead of doing it for ourselves.

So Beverly and I work on strengthening her self-worth and rebuilding her life with different people in it. She can't control Paul or his feelings, but *she can control not being reliant on him for her happiness*. This way, she can drop the need to try to force him to change his mind. Our personal responsibility is to feel and express our pain or fears without trying to change The Other, or use them as a prop to stop us feeling that pain or fear.

And by letting go of needing to force Paul to change, he won't feel under pressure from Beverly. By not pressurizing him to change, Beverly shows respect for his point of view, even though she completely disagrees with it and is struggling in grief. Beverly's task is to understand herself, respect herself, and love herself.

Coping with heartbreak

If Beverly's situation echoes your own and you love someone who sadly doesn't feel the same way, understand that relationships are way more complicated than simply trusting to a set of rules. This is because The Other is in the relationship too, and you can't control The Other. You can only control the way you behave and react. Keeping busy is a good way to combat times when the end of a relationship leaves you feeling worthless.

Channel your hurt or anger into energy for new activities, such as exercise, which releases feel-good endorphins. Kick-boxing, for example, is a fantastic way to release pent-up anger. This will encourage feelings of worthiness and attractiveness to be self-generated.

Top Tip
Avoid begging the person you adore to stay or come back. This means respecting their position, which is gracious, but it's also far less demeaning for you. This way, you respect yourself enough to aim to be in a relationship with someone who adores and wants you too.

Broken trust

As much as they often cause us pain, intimate relationships provide us with an opportunity to know ourselves better.

Lisa's letter

I feel trapped. When I was twenty-one at college, I broke up with my boyfriend. I became thoroughly miserable and couldn't get out of bed – I was probably depressed. I did eventually come out of the bad place and went on to have a good career and enjoy a couple more casual relationships. I've been seeing Jeff for five years, and we've talked about marriage, but recently I found out he's been unfaithful with someone at work. I'm distraught at this betrayal and, for my own self-worth, I want to break up. However, I'm terrified of plunging back into that dark place again. How can I avoid another broken heart?

Regards, Lisa

One blessing is that Lisa has already survived one break-up, an experience that might be helpful to her in her current deliberations. True, it was obviously traumatic (she suspects she might have been depressed) and she speaks of it as a dark place, a bad place. Yet she came out the other side, for which I'd love her to feel proud and empowered.

She probably also has a different support structure available today. My observation is that the universe has a funny way of providing just what we need, if only we can trust the process. Lisa's ability to learn from past experience is part of a process that enables us to be open and vulnerable in relationships while at the same time being alert to ways to protect ourselves.

One crucial way to protect ourselves in relationships is to retain a sense of self. We're all familiar with the new couple who are so adoring of, so lost in, so all consumed by each other that they drop existing friends or hobbies or plans. Of course, in the early days, doing things as a new couple is part of the fun. Even sharpening a pencil together is fun. No-one begrudges people getting to know each other better. And new relationships re-invigorate us with new ideas, experiences, and intimacies.

Yet keeping up with our friends, our hobbies, our dreams means *we retain part of what makes us who we are.* This provides us with a source of strength and comfort should the worst happen and the relationship break down. I have a friend who claims his life was saved by being part of a choir. Having enjoyed attending on his own a weekly singing rehearsal throughout his relationship, when his partner sadly died my friend found there was already in place a warm and loving familiar community that met once a week. It was a structure that, as he says, 'got me out of the house once a week, when I'd lost all hope.'

Lisa's sadness is in losing not only a long-term relationship, and the dream of being married and having children with Jeff, but also in losing trust. The feelings will sometimes be overwhelming. It's an episode that makes her question her judgement, her intuition, her intellect, her confidence, her very sanity. She has not chosen this experience.

What she can choose is to reframe that experience in her own terms. The heartbreak at the end of her relationship provides an opportunity for choice: Do I stay and work this through with a man I still love and care for? Or, do I protect myself from further future pain by someone who has betrayed me. In other words, it's about making the choice a positive one either way. Staying might be about saving something long-standing or repairing it instead of it being about being afraid to leave; similarly, leaving might be about self-protection or growth instead of about expressing anger. In this way, we can acknowledge the reality of pain and, at the same time, take control of the choices we make and have compassion for them.

Surviving heartache

If you're like Lisa and you want to avoid heartache, the easiest way is to avoid intimate relationships, completely and forever. Yet the price for this solipsism is that you miss out on all the beautiful life-enhancing things relationships can bring, such as warmth, passion, friendship, hope, and growth. It might not feel like it right now, when you're in daily agony, but from pain comes growth.

It's a shame the metaphor most commonly used is of a *broken* heart and therefore perhaps one which is now weaker, or inferior. I prefer to think of the heart in such circumstances as having been badly bruised. Bruises are incredibly painful and can be knocked again and again. But a bruised body also heals, often stronger than before.

Acknowledge your hurt and pain and soothe yourself with long baths, little treats, and good food to nourish and be kind to yourself. Whether single or in a relationship, maintain a sense of self by developing or retaining some separate interests or friends from your partner.

Top Tip
If you're trying to decide whether to stay or go, turn the
options into positive ones for you, which means that
whatever you decide comes from a strong place.

Being separate together

As one of my clients said recently, 'It's OK occasionally to remember to be "me".' I would go so far as to say that for couples it's
essential to know how to be separate together. For a couple to
be content together, they need room to develop as individuals.
We call this process 'individuation', and it's a vital process for
intimate relationships, whereby two people can come together
without losing themselves. Space in relationships is healthy and
appropriate, even when we formalize our intimate relationships
by moving in together, having a civil partnership or getting
married:

Nigel's letter

*My partner Dave and I celebrated our civil partnership in 2009.
We've always had a good social life, apart from the fact that
whenever we're at a party, Dave spends very little time with me, as
a couple. Whenever I mention it, he snaps that I should toughen
up. We do have separate interests and of course are apart during
the day when we're both at work, so is it so wrong of me to want
us to be seen as a couple when we're out socializing with friends or
strangers?*

Regards, Nigel

What Nigel needs to work out is why socializing separately feels so painful. When Dave is talking to others, it doesn't automatically mean that he's avoiding or ignoring Nigel. Nigel's hurt suggests that there's something he's not getting from the relationship that he believes he should be getting.

Getting our needs met in relationships is complicated not just because each of us is different and has different expectations. Some of us want love and support. Some of us want independence and respect. Some of us want things we've wanted since childhood, without even knowing we want them. We crave the adoration we never got from our parents as children, or we want to punish women, or ensnare Daddy. Some of us expect to be The Prince after a childhood of entitlement; some of us want to banish memories of having no friends at school. Our reasons for staying in a relationship go far beyond fancying someone and going on dates.

My work with Nigel lies in helping him to examine what it is he believes he's not getting from his relationship with Dave. Nigel has always been attracted to Dave's confidence. And what Nigel realizes is that having a partner like Dave is like having a short-cut to popularity. Without realizing it, Nigel thinks that with popularity comes protection from loneliness. Dave is a popular man who at work runs a large team of people. He has good people skills. At parties, Dave is in his element. Nigel enjoys being linked to such a confident, popular man, not least because his childhood was relatively lonely. This is *the unconscious fit of his relationship* with Dave, but it also runs the risk of carrying the seeds of its downfall.

I encourage Nigel to talk to Dave, to express his fears of loneliness. But also to find out how Dave feels. Just as we may not be conscious of why we remain in a relationship with someone and which of our many powerful needs is being met, so The Other may not have a clue about which of their needs are being met either. Just as Nigel used to love that Dave is popular, so Dave is attracted to Nigel because he is loyal and loving. Dave gets on well with lots of people but rarely gets close to them. Nigel gives him the closeness he has lacked in other relationships. However, Dave's popularity and Nigel's closeness, two of the things that attracted them to each other in the first place, are now becoming the things that frustrate each about The Other. These elements are in danger of destroying something good.

How to stand separately together

If you've had a similar experience to Nigel and want things from your relationship that you're not getting, be alert for what you bring from your past to your adult relationships in the present. A healthy relationship is one where each partner grows sufficiently secure in themselves that pursuing new directions (going away on a business trip, starting a new hobby, socializing separately) doesn't pose a threat. Wanting The Other to meet all your needs is not mature; to stand on your own two feet while at the same time being part of a couple takes a lot of conscious effort and self-awareness, but it's healthy and mature.

Identify the emotional needs and longings you wish to be met by your partner. This way, becoming conscious of your needs and longings means you can own them and take responsibility for meeting them yourself.

Top Tip

Develop honest communication in which you both assess what you each want in the relationship. This not only stops you assuming your needs will be provided by The Other, it stops you being resentful towards The Other when that need isn't met.

Living a secret life

Of course, just as too much closeness, too much clinging to one another to get our needs met is unhealthy and stifling and destructive to a relationship, too much separation in a relationship is equally unhealthy.

Helena's letter

I've just discovered that James my husband of ten years is addicted to porn. He's been very distant for some time, shutting himself away from me and our two children in the garden shed in the evenings and at weekends. Eventually, when I asked him about it he said he's been caught trawling sites at work and they're threatening to fire him. I know he's upset at having lied to me, but I feel sick and betrayed about the porn, and also furious that he's jeopardized our family's income. Above all, I've lost my trust in him. Should I stand by him or will he always be untrustworthy?

Regards, Helena

Helena is suffering a cocktail of hurts. Secrets corrode relationships, and discovering an unpleasant hidden side to someone, someone we thought we knew intimately, is highly disorientating. In addition, through the lying and the porn, Helena's husband has been taking energy out of the marriage. All these aspects give rise to a loss of trust. And once broken, trust is hard to repair. It can take years.

The relationship is in crisis. In parallel, Helena needs to examine her own feelings and the couple needs to explore how to move forward. It would be great, too, if James could explore his feelings, to understand why he developed a coping strategy that involved shutting himself away from his family and forming a relationship with porn (although as I've explained elsewhere, people need to be self-motivated to go into therapy or to have in-depth conversations with friends for such communication to be successful).

Helena's question to me is about whether to stay or go. However, she phrases it differently, emphasizing that her choice to go will be linked to whether her husband will break her trust again. This last piece of information is impossible to judge. James – and the millions of people over the centuries in similar trust-destroying situations, who for one reason or another have promised to stop drinking/leave a lover/stop gambling/give up drugs/stop vomiting – may very well believe that he'll be able, for the rest of his life, to keep the promise *never to do it again*. Leaving aside spouses who may make such a promise to buy time, but who never have any real intention of giving up their secret behaviour, James's addiction to porn may have deep roots that need examining and treating. Therefore, if Helena stays *just* because James has promised never to do it again, the power in the survival of the couple rests with The Other.

Instead, Helena's focus must be on whether *she* wants to stay (e.g. because she wants to work at saving/improving the marriage) or go (e.g. because she doesn't want to wait for a second betrayal months or years down the line). She must frame her choice in a way that's positive for her instead of a negative (e.g. she doesn't believe she can survive on her own).

At the same time, by communicating as a couple Helena has a chance both to put her own feelings out there for James to reflect on, and to listen to James's feelings. Without condoning his behaviour, people in James's situation behave as they do for specific reasons. Sometimes the reason has nothing to do with the couple; it could be a legacy from the past such as attacking a controlling mother or detached father. It could be now-specific, such as a personality clash at work or struggling with what it means to be a parent or a spouse.

And sometimes it may be to do with the intimate relationship itself, or any grooves or habits that have formed and which it takes a crisis to expose. Sometimes when we've been desperately hurt, the hardest thing for us to acknowledge is our part in the dynamic.

And sometimes couples are put under pressure by simply being a couple. Lovers, porn, lap-dancers, booze or binge-eating offer us the possibility of the buzz of having a secret, the alluring bubble of lust or addiction, the illusion of control or the unspoken attack on The Other. Some people crave the security or stability of marriage *at the same time as* feeling suffocated by its safety and consistency.

Helen understands that since the arrival of children, she and James have led increasingly separate lives. To repair things, they have couples counselling and also plan to spend at least one night a week out together, to reconnect again as a couple. James meanwhile attends a weekly group for porn addiction and initiates a 'computer protocol' so that his shed/office is off limits in the evenings.

Repairing trust

If Helena's situation echoes your own and you've discovered that your partner has been leading a secret life, talk with your partner immediately, to share your feelings. Together, identify how much of their secret life is about your joint relationship and how much is about things at work or about trying to deal with things from their past.

Have the courage to use a crisis to explore yourself and your own behaviour. Only by improved self-awareness can you hope to challenge your fears, inadequacies or insecurities instead of getting upset that your Significant Other is failing to read your mind and maybe repair your damage. Anything else is just sleepwalking through your own relationship.

Top Tip
Examine your own feelings and ambitions and frame your choice, to go or stay, in ways that are positive for you. This way, your choice will come from a place of confidence.

Clashing values

Not all intimate relationships reach crisis point. Some just muddle along with their own particular dysfunctional repertoire.

Lee's letter

I've always been careful with money and assumed that my fiancée Pippa was too because, when we met, Pippa was a single parent living on very little money. Now we both have decent jobs she's become over-generous, giving her sister and parents money to the point of having to borrow from me. She and I row about it all the time. I say we should be saving for our wedding and our future and am now panicking we'll never achieve financial security or have enough money to have more children. How can I get Pippa to tighten her belt – which will soon be ours!

Regards, Lee

A useful exercise for couples is to carry out a *value audit*, which I explain below. Relationships can survive, can even be enhanced by, numerous differences: in hobbies, income, faith, race, even heights. But values underpin who we are. They provide the bedrock to our identity. Couples who plan to have children usually discuss their dreams of how to raise them, as a joint enterprise. So why wouldn't we have similar discussions about how each of us values fidelity, politics, honesty or financial security?

As well as getting Lee and Pippa to do the value audit below, I work with Lee to explore how giving Pippa money is contributing to the problem. When Pippa was a single parent and money was tight, she was careful with her finances. Now she has more money, she needs to learn how to manage her own financial affairs. However, Lee's bailouts are preventing this from happening.

We call such behaviour 'collusion'. Lee claims to be annoyed by Pippa's behaviour, but at the same time his bailouts are supporting her wish to be generous. Parents everywhere will be familiar with Pester Power, when children make a scene to get something bought. Keeping a firm line can be very difficult in the face of tears or tantrums. Lee needs to hold a similarly firm line, not just because financial stability is a healthy way of living, but because he can't complain about Pippa's behaviour if he's similarly weak-willed in the face of her demands for extra cash. We are spectacularly imitative creatures, so Lee needs to model for Pippa the kind of responsible money-management he wishes she'd follow.

Of course, the other thing to say is that in my line of psychotherapy, money rows are very often *not* about the money itself. Often, rows about 'financial supplies' can, below the surface, be about 'emotional supplies', such as feeling secure or being supported enough. Lee reveals how Pippa's spending money on her family makes him feel insecure, knowing Pippa has more people in her life she wants to indulge rather than just Lee and her daughter. On some level, Lee is worrying: is there enough love in this relationship to go round.

It turns out that feeling understood and loved come top on Lee's list of cherished values in a relationship, whereas for Pippa (especially after a few tough years as a single Mum) it's things like laughter and fun. It also turns out that Lee worries that the future is unknown and therefore scary, whereas Pippa, who has survived the hardships of being a single parent, believes she can survive what life throws at her.

Above all, by focusing on *his* list of key values, Lee is better able to determine whether in his relationship with Pippa his underlying values of love and support and understanding and security are shared or even respected. And it also gives Pippa the opportunity to see how her behaviour is affecting someone else, which in turn gives her the opportunity to decide whether or not to change.

The value audit

If Lee's story sounds familiar and you're having repeated rows in your relationship about things that are important to you, do a value audit with your partner. Have the two of you (but separately) draw up a list of all the elements you regard as essential for a mutually satisfying relationship. You can make up the list of values yourself, but they usually include things like trust, respect, tactility, sex, love, money, shared politics, having kids, importance of the wider family, financial security, religion/faith, and sense of humour. Then, again in private, rank them in order of importance.

Come together and compare the two lists. This will help you start a non-confrontational dialogue about the things that matter to you most. And, because of the ranking system, both of you can see at a glance what matters most to the other person. From conversations around this audit, you'll be in a better position to work out whether your partner shares or can even accommodate your values – and whether this is a deal-breaker for you.

Top Tip
Work out whether you contribute to your partner's annoying habits or behaviour, for example by bailing them out financially, offering second helpings when they're trying to lose weight or driving them home from the pub even though you hate that they drink too much. Try to catch yourself doing it, so you can make a decision to stop.

More sex please

As Beverly found when she and Paul went from being great friends to being lovers, sex can complicate relationships. Sex can provide the most exhilarating experiences too, and it can deepen a good relationship into (ahem) an orgasmic one. But the thing to bear in mind is that *all* relationships change over time and this includes sexual relationships. That amazing, ravishing chemistry and passion when we first meet, that well-known honeymoon period, simply cannot be sustained, no matter how wild or fulfilling the sex life. Sex can deepen relationships. It can become even more fulfilling, even more meaningful. Yet it also runs the risk of becoming more mundane, more of a habit. Some sex lives grind to a complete halt.

Now whenever I write about sex, I always hear from people who want me to know how very happy they are thank you with complete celibacy. That a relationship without sex works for them and their partner. Or that without sex, relationships are better. The first thing I'd say to anyone tempted to repeat such sentiments is that this book is for people who want to *improve* their relationships. If having a celibate relationship genuinely works for you *and* your partner, then I'm thrilled for you.

Discovering that someone is in a happy and mutually fulfilling relationship always makes my day.

But I love good sex, and there are many people out there who do too, and yet who wish their sex lives were somehow more fulfilling, more enjoyable, more frequent. This next letter is for people like them.

Liam's letter

My partner Beth and I have been married a year. We only moved in together properly when we got married because, before then we lived at opposite ends of the country (we met at a conference!). We've always had a great sex life but sadly, just lately we seem to have stopped having sex as frequently as we used to. We're still tactile and loving towards each other, but there's less sex. Is this normal? Maybe my wife has stopped fancying me? It's getting me down, but if this is normal I don't want to create a problem when there isn't one.

Regards, Liam

Liam has two areas of concern. One is the decline in the amount of sex with Beth, and the second relates to his interpretation that this might mean she's going off him. We often carry inside a benchmark of what might constitute 'normal' sex. This benchmark can be influenced by our experiences, or by articles we've read or even interviews we've heard celebrities give, gushing about their bedroom activities. There's a belief that there's a 'norm' out there and that, if we aren't achieving it, we've failed in some way.

Over time, couples often find that they experience a deeper sexual experience even as the frequency declines. A case of quality, rather than quantity. However, this either isn't Liam's experience or he hasn't looked at it in this way before. His previous

experience with Beth has perhaps led him to imagine that
there's only one version of perfect sex, and that if this has
changed now, then maybe something has gone wrong in the
relationship.

Now, sex in a relationship is an exquisite form of communication. It doesn't have to be all about penetration or orgasm, since
it also involves sensual touch and reciprocal gestures. It's about
giving and receiving pleasure. It's about growing in tune with our
partner. Liam reports that he and Beth are still loving and tactile
with each other. The question is, is this enough?

Ironically, when you think that sex is about putting our
private parts into someone else's private parts, we're often highly
squeamish when it comes to just *talking* about sex with our
partner. So I urge Liam to start talking to Beth about their sex
life (is she enjoying it, does she wish it was more frequent, are
there things she'd like him to try?) and to start revealing his own
feelings and ambitions for their sex life.

Having decided that more sex would be great, Liam and Beth
start to explore Tantric sex. Tantric sex prolongs sensual intimacy
and deepens sensual bliss. It's about respecting your and your lover's body, worshipping each other's bodies and above all taking the
pressure off sex becoming a 'numbers game'. Rather than complicated techniques, it's about touching and licking and murmuring
and cradling and sucking and stroking. It doesn't have to be about
penetration or climax. If orgasm is achieved, that's a glorious
bonus, but it's not the only goal.

Neither does it have to be about swinging from the chandeliers
dressed only in a thong, or leaping off the wardrobe dressed as
batman – although both, I'm reliably informed, are exceptionally
enjoyable.

Liam has noticed that the change has occurred since getting
married and moving in together. An element of mystery has been
lost. What once was a rare thrill to glimpse each other naked is

now an everyday occurrence. So I suggest Liam and Beth discuss their relationship. *Newlyweds often resist doing this,* believing that they've only just got married so everything must be fine/perfect. In fact, milestone changes, such as formalizing our relationship, even if it's just moving in together, can bring up all sorts of issues in people, around things like identity or fears for the future, or simply around things being different to how we imagined them to be.

From their conversations, Liam learns that Beth is feeling stressed by all the well-intentioned people asking when they might expect the patter of tiny feet. Without realizing it, Beth has begun to see sex as stressful instead of pleasurable. The new Tantric ideas of focusing on sexual pleasure rather than solely penetrative sex means that Beth can process her pregnancy anxieties while discovering new non-penetrative techniques for intimate pleasure. And Liam, of course, is deeply relieved to discover that Beth hasn't stopped fancying him.

Having great sex

If you're like Liam, and you're worried about a change in your and your partner's sex life, remember that sexual intimacy is a form of communication within a couple. Talk sensitively to each other about sex in general and your sex life in particular, which will help you be less self-conscious about the subject. Explore new positions or times of day or locations. Sex isn't about recreating the same excitement that existed at the beginning of your relationship, but about maintaining a sexual journey, which fulfils and nourishes you and your partner.

At the same time, be sensitive to the idea that changes in your sex life can sometimes be a sign that some underlying stressor in your relationship would benefit from being raised and discussed.

Top Tip
Talk to your partner, in and out of bed, about your ideal romantic setting. Create sensual rituals in your bed or bathroom, with candles, music or essential oils. Take the pressure off penetrative sex or reaching orgasm by doing other intimate and tactile things like touching, licking, murmuring, cradling, sucking and stroking, and touch each other with different fingers. This way you'll bless your love life with positive intention.

Self-awareness

To make good choices for yourself in life you need to know yourself fully, and understand what it is you want – not perhaps the thing or the person itself, but what they represent. Above all you need to take responsibility for your actions (your porn addiction, your anger, your passivity) and understand why, for example, you choose to stay stuck or repeat your behaviour like Ed and his affairs.

Fear of loneliness runs deep in our psyche. After all, we're group creatures. We see loneliness as stigmatizing, and try to avoid it at all costs (see Chapter 9, 'Social Media'). And sometimes this propels us into inappropriate relationships, relationships that are unhealthy, *relationships in which we wither rather than flourish*. We can leave, and yet we're terrified of leaving. This is all part of the journey of self-knowledge.

And there is one other thing to bear in mind: life is all about endings. In nature there is decay and dying all around, but there is re-growth too. Or as Leonard Cohen once wrote: there is a crack, a crack in everything. That's how the light gets in.

CHAPTER 5
Siblings

Siblings, if we have them, can provide some of our most enjoyable, enduring relationships and, as a result, can become the crucial anchor-people in our lives. Even though children are aware of their parents and may interact together, child with adult, it's only siblings who experience our childhood as a fellow child.

So I feel almost churlish for daring to mention Cain and Abel. Yet siblings can also give rise to great distresses or resentments, which, similarly, can last a lifetime. Though siblings are usually raised by the same two parents, there are various dynamics – such as parental favouritism or sibling rivalry – that can disturb these relationships and make the shared family unit a radically different experience for each child. Just because siblings share genes, once shared a house and holidays, perhaps were once made to share toys, doesn't mean that they automatically get on.

Sibling rivalry

Conflict arises from the fact that siblings in a family from the very outset compete for limited resources, namely parental attention. I believe that *love is infinite, and that there's always more than enough love to go round*. But attention and hands are a different matter. One parent cannot be tucking up more than one child in bed at any one time. Even if only for a minute, another child is often getting the attention we not only want but feel (in our self-centred, childlike way) is what we deserve.

The extraordinary thing is that sibling respect for birth order, and the privileges or otherwise that stem from where you sit in the familial firmament, seem deeply imprinted.

Claire's letter

I'm the eldest of three children and run a successful team of forty people. I'm well respected in my industry, but as far as my family is concerned it's as if I've achieved nothing. When I rang my mother to tell her my team had won a prestigious government grant, all she wanted to talk about was my brother and sister and their children. I'm not married and I know my mother disapproves of this, but I feel I'm invisible. But now my elderly mother's unwell, my siblings insist I rush over at weekends to help care for her, because they're too busy with their kids. I resent being the reliable oldest one, especially as my mother has always been critical of my 'single' life. How can I make everyone see me differently and pitch in to help?

Regards, Claire

Siblings are acutely conscious of who is getting what parental attention, and whether the treatment (especially the treats) is fair. Claire is alert for her mother talking about her siblings (her rivals) and feels that her own achievements are ignored. Yet when they need her, her family is quick to criticize her lack of involvement.

As the eldest, Claire will have been acutely aware of her 'dethroned' position. There are apparent compensations to being the firstborn: people make a fuss of the Big Sibling. Well-meaning people buy compensatory toys. And over time we may develop a sense of superiority because of being first. But make no mistake, if we had our way, our sibling – or even worse, siblings – wouldn't exist.

Claire and I look at how, in families, we unconsciously adopt roles. Partly this is to deal with the craving for parental attention. It's pointless competing head-to-head with a sibling in terms of being sweet, or mathematical or tidy, because there's every chance (especially if they're older and therefore possess more skills) that they'll be better at it than us. A plan with more chance of success is to work out where the gaps are in the family system, and aim for them.

Claire needs to acknowledge how much she has combined being competent with detaching from her family, because of feeling criticized and ignored. She also needs to see that it's her competence that makes the family turn to her in a crisis.

I ask Claire to think about what she might have gained in the past from such 'good', people-pleasing behaviour. Did she earn praise at home or school? Did the praise offset her guilt about secret resentments towards her rivals? Did she hope 'good behaviour' would make people like her more, such as her mother who has strong views about how Claire leads her life?

Claire's resentments at current family dynamics suggest that she has long been craving parental attention. Claire's dream that her siblings will care for their mother is really her attempt to address the ongoing unfair distribution of emotional supplies. It gives her the strength to talk to her mother about how much she's prepared to do, but also to set limits around her availability, which will force other siblings to contribute.

Managing resentments

If Claire's story echoes yours, and you resent your parents' disinterest, or you feel unfairly treated compared with your siblings, think about your relationships within your family and explore whether your life choices have been driven, perhaps without realizing it, by the need to compensate for a lack of emotional support in childhood. Learning to understand this about yourself means you have the opportunity to be less affected by the apparent unfairness in the present. Also be boundaried in your availability, so that family responsibilities can be shared equally now you're all grown-ups.

Top Tip
Work out your needs as an adult, and aim to provide them yourself. For example, if you still crave affirmation, give yourself praise or rewards/treats – not just for your achievements, but for being you.

Birth order (1)

In terms of human development, positive parental attention endows us with warm feelings of security. This sense of security encourages healthy self-esteem to flourish. If we're the firstborn, we occupy the deliciously privileged position of being the sole object of parental adoration. But this nirvana comes crashing down when siblings arrive. Our life is now populated by rivals.

Younger siblings have one advantage in the bun-fight of family relationships: they've always known family life to include siblings. They usually develop a particular resilience that stems from arriving into a system that already contains rivals. The firstborn doesn't have this luxury.

Our birth order in the family can greatly influence our behaviour and mood, and issues around it can linger well into adulthood.

Eliza's letter

I'm the middle child of three. We've always been close, although I've always hated being in the middle because I have to mediate between family members when there's a row. But now my mother

has let slip that my sisters have fallen out, but no-one has said any-
thing to me. I'm devastated and hurt and feel like cutting ties with
them all. It's as if they can't trust me with the information. What
can I do to make them talk to me about this?

Regards, Eliza

The language of Eliza's letter reveals the depth of emotion triggered by a feud that is, in fact, between two other people. She
feels so rejected by them that she longs to retaliate in kind, by
cutting them out of her life completely.

Eliza's reason for hating being the middle child doesn't quite
ring true. 'Family mediator' is a compelling role to obtain, because
the implication is that such people are above conflict. It's a
position of power, because people turn to the mediator without
judgement or rancour for advice and support.

And when Eliza discovers that her traditional role 'in the middle'
has been ignored, she panics. Part of her identity (more than she realizes) is wrapped up in being 'in the middle', the person who knows
what's going on in the family. Now the family game is being played
differently, Eliza feels unsafe, abandoned. She interprets this to mean
that her siblings don't trust her with the information. In other words,
they're making a mistake, which must be corrected. Above all, she
turns to me to see how she can wriggle back into the middle, her
place of familiarity and therefore safety.

It is possible Eliza's mother is also unsettled by this development in family dynamics. Maybe this prompted her to tip off Eliza
about the feud. This sounds like a family under-skilled or under-
practiced at keeping boundaries. Personal business has to become
everyone's business. There are few private spaces.

With Eliza we explore what makes her feel safe and unsafe. She
tells me of a memory from childhood when she overheard her two
sisters gossiping about her. For Eliza, being in the middle means
being in control, since knowledge is power.

What is crucial for Eliza to recognize is that two siblings falling out isn't anything to do with her. She wants to make it her business because the alternative (being kept out of the loop) feels as though she has lost control. If she can't control what they say to each other, then she won't be able to control what they may say about her.

To have the courage to stay in the background and let the feud run its course is hard for Eliza because it brings up feelings of being left out and out of control. At one point she has to delete the pre-set numbers for her sisters in her mobile to make it harder for her to ring them. Yet over time, Eliza is able to set firmer boundaries for herself – and for other people.

Setting parameters

If Eliza's story resonates for you, and you have panicked that members of the family are not including you in their lives, explore your own history around why it's important for you to be so involved. How did you like to get parental attention? Children are extremely canny at working out what parents like (peace and quiet, cooking, jokes) and quickly develop new skills to ensure parental engagement. Out of this often comes inadvertent favouritism, which as kids we partly orchestrate.

By seeing what you wanted as a child, you'll be able gain a sense of perspective as an adult. By stepping back from family dramas you'll also be in a better position to set boundaries in your life and focus on your own issues, not those of others.

Top Tip
Identify what role you play in your own family, what you gain from this role, and ask yourself how you would feel if you lost this role.

Birth order (2)

It's hard, when we've carved out a family role or had it thrust upon us, not to slip into that role when we find ourselves back in familiar family territory. Christmas, for example, is a classic time when we return home with good intentions only to find ourselves sucked back in to the old patterns of behaving, the old interactions, the old conflicts. Collectively, the way we lapse into old patterns of behaviour when with our family members makes it doubly hard for either side to overcome ingrained prejudices.

Caroline's letter

I'm thirty-five with four older brothers. My siblings want me to have our father move in with me and my family. I make a modest living from sculpture, which I love but all my life my brothers have pushed me around. As a child I was a day-dreamer and they used me as the butt of all their games. Now it frustrates me that my siblings only see the old me who can be pushed around. What can I do to get them to treat me as an adult?

Regards, Caroline

It seems to me that day-dreaming was not just an early sign of the immensely creative person Caroline would become, but an attempt to escape an often intolerable home life in which Caroline was 'the guinea-pig' for the boys. Developing Caroline's self-esteem has been crucial, as she has a tendency to regress, to play the baby of the family. Yet as in any relationship, when we try to change, this becomes an 'unknown' for the people around us, which scares them. They might re-double their efforts to put us back in our pigeon-hole.

In her relationship with these multiple Others (her siblings), Caroline works hard at nourishing her self-worth, through her interactions with friends, her partner and daughters, and her work achievements. Strengthening her self-worth makes it easier for her to confront her brothers.

We also have to unpick the fact that any bullying by the brothers resurrects painful memories of exclusion and loneliness in Caroline's childhood. For years, Caroline has agreed to their wishes, in an unconscious hope that she will one day earn their acceptance.

An unexpected consequence of Caroline's improved self-confidence is that Tom later apologises for their treatment of her in childhood – a magical conversation Caroline never dared imagine would happen.

This is a reminder that the tensions of childhood don't have to last a lifetime but with good, honest communication can be processed and learned from. Caroline and Tom in particular now have a warm intimacy as adults that never existed when they were children. We could say that they're getting to know each other all over again, with added maturity. They've discovered they have many things in common, not just genes.

Because the siblings' initial instruction that Caroline should take in their father was really a hangover from their childhood bullying, once Caroline develops her assertiveness, this matter falls away without further family debate.

Rewriting the family script

If Caroline's story resonates for you, and you're constantly wishing your family would treat you as the adult you are now instead of the child you were then, you need to work on your self-esteem so that their attempts to take you back to the past fail. Surround yourself with good friendships and good activities and don't worry about trying to please your family all the time. It's not about getting your siblings to meet your needs, it's about defining yourself and acquiring the self-confidence to take your own needs seriously.

Top Tip
Shed the label you were given in childhood, such as 'the baby', 'the lazy one' or 'the naughty child', by consciously working hard to overturn that description at every opportunity. This will give you a more adult way of functioning in the world, which in turn will strengthen your assertiveness.

Fighting over toys and boys

The constant sibling competition of the nursery can shape our grown-up conduct.

Nikki's letter

My sister Ashlyn and I are in our late twenties. After Ashlyn broke up with her boyfriend a few years ago, I continued to socialize with Callum, Ashlyn's ex. Unfortunately, my sister has now found out and has hit the roof. She got my mother to tell me to promise that I'll stop socializing with her ex. This has made me absolutely furious, because I knew Callum before Ashlyn did and we always got on really well. In fact, we even dated briefly. I love my sister and I don't want to hurt her, but neither do I want to lose my connection with Callum.

Regards, Nikki

This kind of situation is deeply coloured by issues that have festered since childhood. At the centre of it are two women who ask their mother to mediate just as they would have done as children. There's almost something of the nursery about the way in which Ashlyn ropes her mother in to tell Nikki to stop seeing Callum. At the same time, 'I knew him before she did' sounds like a tantrum-throwing toddler, claiming the toy 'is mine'. In other words, Callum is the latest toy the two women are fighting over.

Despite growing up with each other, the two sisters haven't developed the sophisticated interpersonal skills that can be acquired during childhood conflicts. The 'Running to Mummy' solution suggests that this is what the girls have always done. And no doubt their mother colludes in this, taking the role of referee. Perhaps it makes their mother feel useful. Or maybe it lessens her guilt that her daughters fight, which is why she still acts as the referee even though the girls are adults.

Parental involvement can unwittingly contribute to sibling conflict. Parents are desperate for their kids to get on, but by always resolving disputes, they leave their children under-prepared for negotiating conflict as adults.

Though I explore this in more detail in Chapter 2 ('Parents'), the first thing Nikki and I do is to determine that for her to behave in a mature way she needs to remove her mother from the equation. Otherwise, the childhood dynamics are simply being repeated in the present. Without using her mother as a decompression chamber, Nikki must take responsibility for her own fury.

I also ask Nikki to examine her need to keep Callum in her life. No-one wants to be told who they can and can't socialize with, so this fury could be about feeling controlled. It could also be about whether the relationship with Callum is a way for Nikki to keep something her sister no longer has, like a favourite toy from the past. I also ask Nikki to be honest about how she felt about her sister dating Callum after she did. Can these two girls fully separate? Or does the row over Callum demonstrate how enmeshed the sisters are?

Above all, Nikki needs to talk openly with Ashlyn. It is possible that Nikki's ability to maintain good relations with an ex demonstrates maturity, something Ashlyn might learn from. Once there is proper communication between the two girls, their hostility lessens and a natural affection emerges. With Ashlyn more in her life, Nikki doesn't even feel the need to see Callum so much, and when she does see him, Ashlyn is surprised to feel less jealous.

Taking responsibility

If Nikki's story resonates for you, and your parents are still mediating in disputes between you and your siblings, it's time for you to take responsibility for your behaviour or emotions instead of using your parents as a buffer. Step back and question whether you really want something, or whether you only want it because your sibling has it. Make a note of what emotions your siblings bring up in you. Concentrate on living your life so that you don't have to be so affected by what your siblings get up to.

Top Tip
Catch yourself in the moment behaving as if you and your sibling are still in the nursery, which will give you the opportunity to choose to behave differently.

Twins

Of course, some siblings are with each other from the moment of conception. Twins occupy a unique and fascinating place in the spectrum of relationships. There are two types of twins. Identical twins look similar, share 100 per cent of their DNA, and are always of the same sex; fraternal twins look less alike, grew in the womb from separate eggs, and can be of the same or different sex. Studies have shown that even when raised separately, identical twins will often speak of feeling that something is missing. This reminds us that twins have months of experience together in the womb, while their senses are developing, before they meet anyone else in the world.

Lola's letter

I've always wanted to get away from Caz. I hated the way every-one treated us as one person, dressed us alike, put us in the same class at school, bought us the same things for birthdays. At seven-teen I left home, went off the rails, took a drug overdose in Cambodia and was attacked in Brazil. I wanted to feel things as me, and not us. Caz wishes we were closer, but this only makes me run away from her even more. When she married, she wanted me to be her bridesmaid and I had to pretend to be in some remote part of India, unable to get home. I feel suffocated as her twin. I don't know what to do.

Regards, Lola

Lola's experience reminds us that all relationships need healthy not fuzzy boundaries. We need a sense of our Self, our individuality, otherwise we become enmeshed in The Other. Being enmeshed is a confused, unhealthy place to be. We all have to learn to separate from the mother, which is a complex developmental process, but twins must also negotiate the separating from 'we' to 'I' as well.

Lola's need for boundaries seems to stem as much from her sister Caz's need for closeness as from her own craving for something more autonomous. Her extreme reaction to Caz's bridesmaid request shows how deep is her resistance to being part of Caz's world. Lots of twins adore being a twin. They speak of the fun they had as children, feeling understood, playing jokes by swapping places, and generally having a positive experience. Lola's constant travelling suggests that not even the world provides a big enough gulf between her and her twin.

Yet it's also a sign of Lola's healthy need to be treated as an individual and not as a unit, a sign of her rejection of only one aspect of her identity (that of 'twin-ness'), and a need for the outside world to fully affirm who she is. The end result of not attending the wedding is people asking 'where's Lola?' She becomes more noticeable by her absence.

In this way, we see that Lola is both angry at Caz and at the world. Lola projects her frustrations about the predictable way other people treated 'the twins' onto Caz. It's as though she imagines people treated the twins as a unit because they favoured Caz. This hands Caz all the power, which in turn gives Lola her constant excuse to look for ways to escape. 'Escape' and 'absence' become Lola's primary way to experience herself as an individual.

Defining yourself

If Lola's story echoes yours, and you're frustrated at being a twin, write down what you feel makes you who you are, including any negatives as well as all the positives. Surround yourself with people who respect you and allow you to flourish. Not only will this strengthen your sense of Self, it will help you better process lingering anger or resentments. At the same time, acknowledge how your twin feels. If you feel able to speak to them, navigate a path of mutual respect, although you may have to settle ultimately on agreeing to disagree about the joys or otherwise of being a twin.

Top Tip
To combat fuzzy boundaries, write down what makes you feel 'you', values that might include respect, dignity, honesty, and loyalty, together with how you feel about politics, fashion, food or music. Defining yourself is a crucial step in taking responsibility for your life and choices.

The witness to our childhood

Only children imagine that having a sibling would provide them with someone to corroborate their own experiences – someone to bear witness to their childhood and agree on any interpretations about it. However, siblings do not always provide such companionship or relief – quite the opposite in fact. A common cause of resentment in adulthood is this imbalance of experience.

Andrew's letter

My older brother Adam was the apple of our Dad's eye. No matter how many scrapes he got into at school, he was never punished. However, Dad was always violent towards me, and I have a vivid memory that when I failed to get top marks in a maths test, my Dad beat me. Now my father is ill – Adam tells me he's dying – but I'm reluctant to get involved. Adam is angry I haven't visited the hospital, and rings me to remind me what a great Dad he was. This

only makes me more angry because this isn't my experience of the
man. How can I get my brother to see my point of view?

Regards, Andrew

As you can imagine, Andrew and I do a lot of work processing
his pent-up anger and sadness towards his Dad, around the man's
violence and apparent parental favouritism. But his story also
provides a stark illustration of one of problems in sibling relationships, which occurs when siblings are not able to corroborate each
other's experience.

Andrew has one view of his father and Adam has a completely
opposite view of the same man. What Andrew really wants is for
his brother to verbally acknowledge that their childhoods with
the same man felt radically different for the two sons, and to perhaps understand Andrew's dislike of their father. But that means
trying to change Adam, which is inappropriate.

Andrew eventually agrees to visit his Dad in hospital with the
trade-off that Adam agrees to a separate meeting alone with
Andrew. Andrew's meeting with his Dad is brief. He sits at the
bedside of an old man dying of emphysema, and silently in his
head, acknowledges his regret that the man couldn't be the Dad
of his dreams. Afterwards, at the meeting alone with Adam, in a
busy wine bar opposite the hospital, Andrew tells Adam about his
memories of the man and of their joint childhood. After the
meeting, Andrew laughs with me that even though his brother
failed even for a second to understand or agree on his point of
view, Andrew has gained comfort from the fact that he had the
courage to articulate his own experience to his brother.

Andrew and I also look at understanding that Adam had
always been the preferred son, but how this wasn't Adam's fault.
By processing his jealousy of Adam, Andrew finds he no longer
needs to be angry with Adam for not sharing the same perspective
of those years.

Acknowledging your experience

If Andrew's story resonates for you, and you and your siblings cannot agree on what your shared childhood experience was like, acknowledge your version of your childhood, and any hurt or pain you felt. Although it's always reassuring to receive feedback that chimes with our own experience, learn that taking your own experiences seriously can still make you feel held and understood.

Avoid blaming the favoured sibling in your family, and try to understand that this position was not of their making. This will help you manage any residual resentment you may feel that they received something from your parents (attention, praise, kindness) that you didn't receive.

Top Tip

Give yourself permission to feel differently about your childhood from your sibling(s). By taking your experience seriously, you affirm your right to be heard – even if only by yourself.

Step-siblings

Step-families only arise out of trauma, especially from a child's perspective. Step-families might represent a joyful union and closure after pain for the adults, but they come into existence when either a parent dies or an existing family is ruptured in some way. This gives rise to anger and resentment. Not surprisingly, the blending of two families can seriously affect sibling dynamics.

Gary's letter

My step-sister Jill and I are only 17 months apart and all our lives my mother (her step-mother) has encouraged us to get on. We have very different interests, very different personalities, and are really only in each other's lives because my mum and her dad got married, forcing two only-children to become siblings. It's got to the point now where we just about manage to send a text on each other's birthday, and be civil to each other at family gatherings. The thing is, I'm not interested in her or her life. Should I try to be her friend?

Regards, Gary

As adults, Gary and Jill don't hate each other but there's a lack of intimacy that has never been properly addressed. Paternal attempts to force siblings to get on often backfire as children enjoy finding ways to rebel. And because this has always been the case for Gary and Jill, they remain unskilled as to how to get on or forge a bond that never existed.

When Gary wonders whether he ought to become Jill's friend, he makes it sound like an obligation. Therapists get very twitchy at what is known as 'the tyranny of the shoulds and oughts'. These words strangle our own choices, and require us to behave according to someone else's wishes.

Not surprisingly, Gary has absolutely no idea how Jill feels about the situation. They've managed for thirty odd years without raising the subject. And even if Jill would love a closer relationship, Gary is quick to point out that she's made little effort over the years to engage him.

Gary and I look at what would be a more authentic relationship for him with Jill. He has a fantasy that his mother dies and they give a joint speech at her funeral. When I suggest that this sounds as though he feels he needs to 'de-throne' his mother before he can create a more realistic relationship with his step-sister, he remembers that years ago, his mother asked him to pay off some of Jill's debts, which Gary hugely resents.

We explore his feelings towards the creation of the step-family and his frustrations at being forced to do things as a unit, a myth he'd always wanted to puncture. Once Gary has permission to acknowledge his negative feelings towards childhood events, he finds himself in a better position to think about forging a relationship with his adult step-sister – on his own terms. They aren't friends, and they're unlikely ever to be so, but he's prepared to explore whether he can forge a realistic sibling bond outside the more structured family gatherings.

Adult negotiations

If Gary's story has echoes for you, and you are wondering whether to engineer an improved relationship (or any relationship at all) with your step-sibling, take yourself back to when your step-family was created. What were your feelings then, and how – if at all – were your feelings acknowledged by the grown-ups.

Once you've processed these old feelings, your feelings in the present day about your step-sibling may change. You may, for example, be able to see them as an adult instead of a child who came unasked for into your life. Assess what kind of relationship, if any, you want with your step-sibling, and check whether you want this for you, rather than simply to please someone else.

Top Tip

Consider talking to your step-sibling to determine whether they have a concern about the quality of your mutual relationship. This conversation can act as the first step in forging a bond as adults, which, for one reason or another, hasn't existed before.

Coping with step-families

At the blending together of two families, any only children must rapidly figure out how to live in this brave new sibling-populated world. Conflict over territory can be intense when one family moves into the house of the other family. And if we've got used to our place in the family birth order, this may also change seemingly overnight, giving rise to further resentments.

However, as with most rivalry, it isn't all bad that step-siblings don't always get on. The children now have the chance to experiment with new roles, new relationships, which is always beneficial.

Two-way communication is key here, so that all the siblings can speak of their feelings about the new family unit, and feel heard. New house rules are also vital so that siblings are treated fairly. Children thrust into this new system may never become close friends, but with time and the opportunity for shared experiences, they can develop a sense of being step-siblings, which, over time, may develop into a loving bond.

Unresolved conflict

If tensions or conflicts in sibling relationships are not addressed, they may be played out in the next generation.

Nancy's letter

Between the ages of seven to twelve, I was verbally and physically abused by my brother, Chris. Apart from my mother, I've never told anyone else in my family about this, and even now I'm extremely cautious about attending family gatherings. He and I both have seven-year-old daughters, and now he's suggested that my daughter goes to stay with them so the cousins can get to know each other better. However, my daughter has recently told me that at family parties, her cousin pinches and kicks her. My husband and I are stalling but the wider family are now beginning to ask why we're spoiling our daughter's fun. If I say anything in the family, there'll be fireworks. What on earth can I do?

Regards, Nancy

The idea of her daughter being on Chris's territory appals Nancy. Understandably, she identifies with her daughter, and refuses to put her daughter in a situation even remotely similar to that of her own childhood. So I'm intrigued why Nancy fears that if she explains the reasons for her choice, there will be family fireworks.

'The Other' in Nancy's situation is not just her brother Chris but the whole family, who she fears will close ranks against her and her husband. When I ask her what this would feel like, she weeps to recall how when she went to her mother to complain about Chris's physical bullying, her mother waved her away saying she had to learn to fight her own battles. What haunts Nancy now is that if she 'goes public' within the family about Chris's previous treatment of her in childhood, her mother will again wash her hands of it all. Nancy fears feeling as unsupported as she did as a child. The exasperation in the last line of Nancy's letter hints at her exasperation in childhood.

We focus on getting Nancy to see that even though she felt unsupported and powerless as a child, she is no longer that child. She's an adult, with adult skills and resources, which include a supportive husband. By talking about her anger and frustration over what happened in the past and over her relationship with Chris in the present, Nancy begins to feel more confident about her beliefs and moral code. We look at how physical abuse constitutes completely unacceptable behaviour and how, as a relative,

Nancy is in an appropriate position to challenge her niece's physically abusive behaviour.

We also debate whether speaking out to the family, on behalf of her daughter, is Nancy's way of retrospectively soothing her inner child for not being understood and supported by her mother in childhood. And yet Nancy is clear that it's also her daughter she wants to soothe and support, by taking direct action.

Nancy doesn't beg her brother to speak to his own daughter about her behaviour, which would be giving Chris the power to deal with this problem. Instead, at the next family event, when she comes under pressure again to let her daughter stay with Chris and his family, Nancy stands her ground and tells the gathering that she doesn't approve of children who pinch and kick other children, and that she won't be letting her daughter socialize with her cousin until that changes. Then, turning to Chris she adds that she has never approved of such behaviour, even when Chris was younger. These are sentences that Nancy and I practised over and over again until it felt very natural to her, very authentic, to be setting such boundaries. Instead of the past being re-lived, it is used to re-shape the present.

Addressing secrets from the past

If Nancy's story resonates for you, and secrets remain from your past that have never been addressed, have compassion for your childhood weaknesses, when you were less able to protect yourself. At the same time, identify your strengths and skills as an adult, as well as your support network of friends and maybe your spouse. Practise telling someone, politely yet firmly, that their behaviour was or remains unacceptable. This will give you time to make sense of how you feel, to articulate it in your own words, and to feel confident if or when you decide to speak out to the person concerned.

Top Tip
Work on respecting your Self and your values, and be prepared to assert both. Do this by setting boundaries for yourself, such as around your availability or your sense of what you consider acceptable behaviour from others. This will mean you're taking responsibility for how you allow other people to treat you and your family.

Being a role model

As we live longer and have new relationships and babies in later life, families come into being with wide age gaps between siblings.

Esther's letter

I'm now twenty-seven. When I was thirteen, I dabbled in drugs. My Mum kicked me out when I was sixteen and I lived in a squat for three years. Eventually I met a man, got clean for him, got a good job and worked hard at repairing my relationship with my Mum. Now, my half-sister Eleanor seems to be sliding down the same slippery slope I did. The problem is, she doesn't see me as her sister, more as a very uncool grown-up. How can I pass on my hard-earned wisdom that drugs are bad and that she should concentrate more at school?

Regards, Esther

It occurs to me that Esther is rather playing down her rebellious years, when she talks of dabbling in drugs. For her mother to have kicked her out, things must have been pretty bad. And yet now at twenty-seven it's hard to imagine her racy past. With her good job and steady boyfriend, she comes across as conventional and mature, which might be making it hard for Eleanor to take her warnings seriously.

We look at what was going on for Esther when she rebelled and it becomes clear it was linked to the arrival on the scene of her step-father, Eleanor's dad. The bad behaviour that led to Esther being thrown out of the family home all started when the cosy twosome she had enjoyed with her mother was altered by the arrival of her step-father.

Esther imagines that Eleanor is feeling as lost and confused, as only teenagers can, as Esther once did. By wanting to stop her half-sister making the same mistakes, she's also trying to repair something from her past. As the much older sibling, she has wisdom and experience to share. But for now the age gap means that the girls haven't really connected intimately before, so Esther's advice comes across as too parental and boringly grown-up.

We decide to tackle Esther's quandary from sideways on, and look at ways in which Esther can develop a low-key friendship with Eleanor, without bringing up the issue of drugs or school attendance. By going to the cinema or shopping for clothes, and having stereotypical yet meaningful chats about make-up and periods and boys, Esther and Eleanor have shared experiences as sisters and later as friends.

This is when Esther realizes she had never had anyone to do such things with when she was Eleanor's age. She starts to mention this to her half-sister, which allows Eleanor to gain some understanding as to what life was like for her older sister. Instead of nagging, Esther shows her vulnerable side, which is something Eleanor can identify with. This makes the conversations deeper. Over a short period of time, Eleanor's self-esteem and schoolwork both improve. And Esther discovers a relationship with a half-sister she hadn't realized she's been missing.

Appropriate bonding

If Esther's story sounds familiar, tread respectfully, and beware of offering advice when no relationship exists. If your half-sibling was about to step out into the road into the path of an oncoming car, instinctively you'd leap to stop them. But in life you sometimes have to learn to let people make their own mistakes.

Even so, develop bonds based on kindness and make sure to keep the relationship age-appropriate, and not flood your relative with 'adult' information. Enjoy your time with them and allow any advice to flow naturally. Avoid only talking to them about what they shouldn't do, otherwise they may retreat from you further.

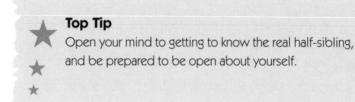

Top Tip
Open your mind to getting to know the real half-sibling, and be prepared to be open about yourself.

Survivor guilt

Sometimes we feel our lives are influenced by our siblings, even when they're no longer around.

Peter's letter

I'm nearly twenty-eight, but I can't seem to get my parents to accept me for who I am. My younger sister Hannah died when she was only a few hours old, and since then I've always felt like the wrong child survived. As a teenager I rebelled by getting in with a bad crowd at school, shoplifting and flunking my exams. But at around twenty something clicked and I started work, saved hard, and now own my own car and flat. But deep down I know my parents are disappointed in me because I'm not their little girl. How can I be happy with my life?

Regards, Peter

Peter suffers a form of 'survivor guilt' whereby he carries the burden that he should have died instead of Hannah. The key thing to note is that even though Hannah died nearly twenty-five years ago, her death has become part of Peter's identity.

One of the earlier things Peter and I explore is whether his parents' disappointment is explicit or assumed, or whether the disappointment is coming from Peter, something he projects onto himself. Peter needs to move out of Hannah's shadow.

To do this Peter needs to strengthen his sense of self to include emphasizing the activities and achievements that could help him value himself – including being proud of having turned his own life around after rebelling in his teens. We also explore whether the things he has achieved, such as maintaining a good job and buying a flat, are what he honestly wants in life, or are they traditional things Hannah might have been expected to do?

At this point Peter recognizes that one of his dreams has always been to travel to Australia and swim at the Barrier Reef. Without realizing it, he has avoided pursuing this dream because he doesn't imagine he's worth it. It's as if his unconscious is nagging him, saying that someone who shoplifts as a teenager doesn't deserve the treat of swimming in the Barrier Reef, or that someone whose sister died young cannot expect to do truly joyful things.

Here we see how the legacy of Hannah's death is still being played out in Peter's present. It is possible that as Peter was barely three years old at the time of Hannah's death, his feelings around her death (loss and sadness, but also guilt and confusion) weren't adequately attended to by the adults in his life at the time.

As Peter grows in confidence, he notices that his parents' comments to him about Hannah are more about trying to remember her, rather than comparing him unfavourably with her. What he'd assumed was their disappointment is in fact their attempts to keep her memory alive. When Peter eventually, nervously, tells his parents about his plans for Australia, his mother bursts into tears – not from sadness but from utter joy, that her son is pushing himself and doing exciting things with his life. They've been worried, it turns out, that Peter had been tying himself down too soon, with the steady job and the car and the flat. Australia is a sign to them that he is now grabbing life with both hands.

Living your life

If Peter's story resonates for you, and the death of a sibling still affects your life, find people to talk to, as other family members may not be so available to you due to their own feelings about the dead person. Identify whether there are any feelings around not having had a longer relationship with this unique and constant figure in your life.

If you're haunted by guilt or a sense that you're a disappointment, examine whether these feelings are coming from a parent or from yourself and your own fears of inadequacy. Work, too, on valuing yourself and strengthening your sense of who you really are. This will help you to step out from the shadow of your sibling and their memory.

Top Tip

Work on letting go of any guilt that 'the wrong child survived' or that you've not adequately lived a life for two people, by each day defining yourself and your ambitions as well as reminding yourself that you have a right to live your life.

The spectrum of sibling relationships

Just because you share a childhood with another child doesn't automatically mean you'll get on, either in childhood or in later life. The general wisdom is that we all have different needs for intimacy, communication, or alone-time, just as we all have different childhoods. But somehow this wisdom gets ignored when it comes to siblings.

At one end of the spectrum, some siblings get on wonderfully, communicate with each other, and enjoy each other's company. At the other end of the spectrum are those who loathe and actively avoid each other. And for certain toxic relationships, avoidance is the best course for all concerned.

But in between those two extremes are siblings who: only connect at family events or when their respective children are playing together; are polite and civil but who make no effort; go through the motions of sending birthday and seasonal cards; and those who are in the same room at family events but can barely speak to each other.

There's always scope for improvement, if that's what you want. I always advise clients who are siblings to explore first whether they want the improvement. If the desire is authentic, there's more chance of finding a way, writing that letter, having that conversation. If we keep coming up with excuses, or keep putting it off, or keep blaming The Other, then maybe deep down our heart isn't in it.

Many siblings find that the predictable life event of a parent's death can act as a trigger for the sibling relationship to move to a new phase. Sadly, it could deteriorate, as with a dispute over a will, for example.

Yet many people find that the shared experience of mourning a parent or other family member can generate enough goodwill and warmth and affection for the relationship to be improved and strengthened. It isn't only in novels and movies and soap-operas that the sibling we always thought of as the 'black sheep' comes back into the fold a changed person, or for siblings to have soul-sharing conversations in the hospital corridor in which feelings are laid bare and the festering air of decades is cleared.

No matter at what age you start, attempting to negotiate a way towards a relationship with a sibling is never wasted energy. Rather, it's a great life lesson for learning to live in a world populated by other people competing with us for the same available resources.

CHAPTER 6
In-laws

Not getting on with the in-laws has been the butt of jokes for centuries. Dreadful mothers-in-law, for example, feature in Chaucer's *The Canterbury Tales*, written as long ago as the fourteenth century. Yet given that often we don't see our in-laws on a daily basis, it's fascinating that relations with them can still be so immensely complex and fraught.

This is because we never choose our relationships with our in-laws. They are foisted on us because they're related to the people we love. As a result, we can't easily ignore them.

'He's mine!'

In an ideal world, our parents love us unconditionally. Our in-laws – if they love us at all – love us much more conditionally, with one eye judging our suitability as a partner for their offspring, and the other eye on how this new partnership threatens what they once had with their child. We're all meant to be grown-ups by the stage we get to be parents- or children-in-law, yet the spirit of the nursery or the playground is never very far away.

Andrea's letter

My mother-in-law is extremely competitive and critical and can't seem to realize that her son has chosen to marry a woman capable of running a home, going out to work, and raising children. I can just about tolerate her digs that I can't cook (my husband and I enjoy cooking together; it's our special time to talk through the day) and her comments that I can't pronounce my husband's Dutch name (I have a degree in languages). Now she wants to take over our tenth wedding anniversary party. My husband has tried talking to her but she refuses to listen, literally covering her ears. My friends laugh because they see their husband as the 'extra child' in their marriage, but in mine the extra, demanding child is my mother-in-law. How can I tell her to back off?

Regards, Andrea

By criticizing Andrea, and trying to muscle in on the wedding party, the mother-in-law is trying to triumph over Andrea to compensate for a reality in which she believes Andrea has won everything. It's not that she doesn't know that Andrea is competent, it's that she knows it only too well. She has been usurped. On some level, Andrea's mother-in-law envies her daughter-in-law (Andrea's life, her youth, her relationship with her husband), and envy is a highly corrosive and destructive emotion.

The behaviour and the hands-over-the-ears suggest that the woman has regressed to childhood. Such women are often in denial about their unpleasant feelings towards their daughter-in-law, and therefore may not understand that deep down they *do* intend to cause hurt. Sadly, what Andrea's mother-in-law may also not be able to see is that by attacking one half of the couple, she may well alienate her son too.

So, as when trying to teach children discipline, Andrea and her husband will need to set kind yet firm boundaries – and be consistent in enforcing them. For example, using rehearsed statements when the mother-in-law goes into one of her critical riffs (such as, 'that statement is both unkind and untrue') mean that the couple are demonstrating a united front.

If she's critical to Andrea in Andrea's home, it's acceptable to explain (the person with the primary relationship, i.e. Andrea's husband, needs to be the one to do this), firmly yet politely, that such ill-mannered behaviour will not be tolerated. This can take time, but united consistency will mean Andrea's mother-in-law will be less able to convince herself that her son is just doing his wife's bidding. Therefore, she'll have less cause to turn to her son hoping for a different outcome.

Strengthening Andrea's sense of self-worth is also important. Although the criticisms about parenting can knock her confidence, if Andrea can strengthen her own faith in her parenting skills, she can detoxify her mother-in-law's criticisms.

Another way of dealing with criticism is to give the woman the benefit of the doubt – or at least pretend to. Andrea asks, as if out of genuine interest, what her mother-in-law would do differently, for example about raising the children. It's an offer to make her mother-in-law feel part of the solution. This gives Andrea the opportunity to reflect on which of the two options she prefers, her idea or that of her mother-in-law, and then choose; as the children's mother, she's the one who must ultimately decide. This way, Andrea regains control of her life, her cooking, and the parenting of her own children, while disarming her mother-in-law with gracious consideration.

At the same time, Andrea feels sorry for her mother-in-law and wants to extend an olive branch. 'Otherwise,' Andrea tells me, 'I'll have sunk to her level.' This puts Andrea in a position to be gracious, for example around the tenth wedding anniversary party. Although the party will still be organized and paid for by Andrea and her husband, it's within Andrea's gift to offer her mother-in-law a task for the party, such as asking her to plan the seating for the guests allocated to her own table.

Disarming the mother-in-law

If Andrea's story echoes yours, and you have a mother-in-law who is hostile or interfering, remember that they probably feel they've lost in the non-existent battle for your partner. Work on understanding that although their barbs feel personal, they're really attacking the idea of you and what you represent. Work on strengthening your self-esteem, reminding yourself that you're a good parent or that your spouse chose you for your many lovely qualities.

You might also consider asking the in-law what they'd do differently in a certain situation – after all, you don't have to go along with their suggestion.

Top Tip
Setting firm boundaries is about taking care of yourself, by putting structures or rules in place for your interactions with others. For example, if your in-law is rude to you or your family, explain that they're not welcome in your home, or that you'll put the phone down. Enlist your partner's support in jointly conveying the boundary. This way you present a united front. Boundaries are not threats. They're about communicating what the consequences will be if someone persists in their difficult behaviour.

Conflicting values

Compromise and accommodation are all very well, but the very nature of in-law relationships can make this tricky.

Aileen's letter

My father-in-law was in the Navy, which is my sorry attempt at
explaining why he's crude and sexist. When I first met him I was
able to turn a deaf ear to his ridiculous comments, but now I have
two daughters aged five and three, I'm nervous they'll pick things
up when they go to stay with Granny and Grandpa. As a result
I've turned down several invitations for them to go and visit and it's
been noticed, but I'm uncomfortable about revealing the real reason. My husband says I'm being over-sensitive but I don't need my
daughters hearing his filth.

Regards, Aileen

The frustrating thing for anyone in Aileen's situation is that
children are like sponges. We have evolved to soak up information during childhood. The children don't know, as the younger
Aileen did, that they have permission to turn a deaf ear to
obscenities. As a result, as much as we try to protect our kids,
we can't prevent them picking up language and ideas from the
television, the playground, even the street.

Again, a united front is the best approach when tackling in-law
issues. Aileen doesn't say what her relationship with her mother-
in-law is like, and her husband only has a brother; if he'd had a
sister, Aileen could be encouraged (hopefully) by how well the
woman turned out despite having such a crude and sexist man for
a father. Maybe Aileen's husband's sensitivity is something along
the following lines: 'I was raised by this man and it hasn't done me
any harm.'

Another tricky aspect to this situation is that things have
changed over the years. This is not to condone sexism or
racism or foul language, but some people don't know – or don't
want to know – that the rest of us have moved on and find
such things disgraceful. Aileen and her husband decide that
he will speak to his father while Aileen sounds out her

mother-in-law. After all, it seems a shame to deprive Granny of the company of her granddaughters just because her husband is a sexist ignoramus.

Aileen feels much more in control now that she can assess whether her mother-in-law is likely to uphold similar standards, disapproving of foul language in front of the children, which might give Andrea comfort for the planning of any future visits. And if she ever believes that her daughters have picked up language from Grandpa, she'll have the perfect opportunity to start conversations with them about how unacceptable such language is, whether it's used by an older relative or whether it's heard in the playground.

Uphold your values

If Aileen's story resonates for you, and you have in-laws who function according to a different moral code to you, recognize that you can't control your in-laws, but you can remain true to your own values. Accept what does and doesn't lie within your control. Encourage your partner to talk to his or her parents; and do it jointly if they're apprehensive. If you have kids, explain to them why certain behaviour is unacceptable, even if their grandparents do it. This way, your stance will show your children that even though they sometimes visit Grandpa, you don't condone his behaviour.

Top Tip
Uphold your values, even if your in-laws are overbearing and hold contrary views. The forced closeness of the in-law relationship mustn't become an excuse for compromising or abandoning your values.

Air-brushing out the rivals

Often what happens in families is that certain behaviour goes un-noticed (or more likely unchallenged) until an outsider arrives. The son- or daughter-in-law is the outsider and their very pres-ence can cause ripples. Some people find the arrival of a son- or daughter-in-law, or even a brother- or sister-in-law so threatening, they try to pretend their rival doesn't exist.

Tim's letter

The couple who would have been my in-laws died before I married their daughter, so I naively assumed I wouldn't experience the horror-in-law stories some of my friends describe. However, my sister-in-law Susanna now feels herself to be the matriarch of the family. On the day I married her sister (I was paying for the wed-ding), Susanna asked me and the two other brothers-in-law to step out of the pictures so that the photos could be of just 'the family'. At funerals, Susanna draws up seating plans for the pews so that her siblings sit around her, while spouses (like me) have to sit apart, unable to comfort our partners. I know from conversations within the family that I'm not alone in finding her behaviour insulting, but my wife is reluctant to rock the boat. Should I say anything?

Regards, Tim

Tim, as the outsider, can see perhaps more clearly the interplay between family members. If we regard families as systems, the same issue can be seen in birth families where, as children get older, they feel compelled to challenge what they see as the dysfunctional dynamics they witness between their parents. These dynamics will have evolved over time, and usually for a reason, such as preserving status or burying resentments. To 'newcomers' to the system, such as children or in this case Tim, the dysfunction seems so glaringly obvious that they can't understand why no-one says anything. The same principle lies behind the story of the little boy in 'The Emperor's New Clothes', who dares to articulate the obvious.

Tim's sister-in-law, Susanna, sounds controlling. Since she's the eldest sibling of four, it's possible that, historically in her family, this was the role which fell to her or which she carved out for herself. This has become part of her identity, and the idea she might lose it causes her to 'act out' her fear, through public displays of having her family close around her, and keeping the 'outsiders' – the rivals – out.

Tim has several options. He can choose to become the spokesperson for the newbie 'faction' of the family system, a faction less tolerant of the ongoing behaviour. Or he could laugh off Susanna's regular manipulations, deriving comfort from the knowledge that he's not alone in thinking her behaviour ridiculous. Or he could decide to address his sister-in-law only when her behaviour impacts directly on him.

A short while after seeing me, he attends another family event and notes that, far from ignoring Susanna's behaviour, her blood relatives do sometimes stand up to her. When she tries to exclude an in-law from a family activity, one of Tim's other sisters-in-law says, 'no Susanna, my husband *is* family.'

Dealing with territorial in-laws

If Tim's story echoes yours, and you have an in-law who wants to squeeze you out, take comfort from the fact that even though the behaviour appears to be targeted at you, it's really a desperate attempt to regain control by someone who is terrified their power is being eroded. In-law conflict is highly territorial. In most cases, the older generation feels threatened by the younger one, but it can get played out between people from the same generation.

Often these people are remembering how cosy life was before all these pesky newcomers rode into town.

In response to such behaviour, coordinate a united front with your partner, and identify who your allies are in the wider family. This will help you feel supported and stop you feeling overwhelmed by the panic of your in-law, The Other.

Top Tip
Set firm boundaries for yourself and your partner and together state (perhaps repeatedly) that certain behaviour is unacceptable. Remember, you have the right to take care of yourself, and setting firm boundaries is the way to do this.

A lack of acknowledgement

Much in-law conflict occurs because the power lines are shifting. The conflict is about this unspoken power struggle. As in all relationships, remaining true to your own values is essential. The in-law relationship must not force you to tip-toe on eggshells around things that go against what you believe in.

Francesca's letter

My daughter and son-in-law don't earn much money, so my husband and I pay for the schooling of their twin boys. We've had much pleasure out of the arrangement, being invited to sports days and so forth, but academically the boys are not performing as we would like. We get sent copies of their termly reports and it's obvious they're notorious around the school for getting into trouble.

As my husband rather grimly said, 'these reports look like my old ones!' I've tried speaking to their parents but my son-in-law just gets defensive, saying they're just being boys and that they'll grow out of it. But I can't help thinking, it's my money! I don't want to fall out with my daughter and son-in-law, but what are my options?

Regards, Francesca

The phrase that keeps coming into my head is, 'He who pays the piper calls the tune.'

Committing to pay for someone's education feels like an investment and we always want to get the best results from our investments. Francesca's relationship with her son-in-law is being tested here. It's possible he feels emasculated by her generosity, and feels uncomfortable that on this issue he's not the manly one providing for his sons. This could explain his defensiveness, and might explain why he hasn't chided his sons about their reports.

The lack of financial investment on his part has also reduced his commitment to this aspect of their upbringing. Even so, this doesn't mean Francesca and her husband need to abandon their values around working hard and respecting the gifts of others, nor their scrutiny of their 'investment'.

I ask Francesca and her husband to (separately) draw up a wish list of all the things they'd hoped originally their grandsons would obtain from this opportunity. Francesca remembers she'd envisaged it as being about more than just academic achievements, but about such things as making friends, great sporting facilities, a rural rather than an urban environment, exposure to the arts, and lots of homework. And she has to concede her husband didn't turn out too badly, despite earning a string of awful school reports.

But the wish list also provides Francesca and her husband with the opportunity to talk about the subject from different angles. In opening up about their shared values around education and discipline, they also share their upset at their son-in-law's casual attitudes to work and providing for their daughter. This isn't necessarily something they can do anything about (their daughter seems happy with her husband) and they refuse to rubbish their son-in-law openly, but together they take private comfort from a shared perspective. My father once joked that God created in-laws specifically to unite otherwise squabbling couples against them.

By discussing the issue, Francesca and her husband see that what they'd expected was 'implied gratitude' from their grandsons in the form of perfect school reports. By discussing the issue next with her daughter (with regard to in-law conflict, it's better that the blood relatives communicate – so long as the relative being talked to doesn't try to diminish the conversation by attributing it to the absent in-law), it's clear Francesca's daughter isn't aware of how disappointed her parents are. Since the children aren't going to show their appreciation properly, it's up to Francesca's daughter and husband to make up the shortfall of gratitude. This they start to do not just with small gifts or thank you letters, but somehow their son-in-law is galvanized into disciplining his sons.

Accommodating different rules and values

If you empathize with Francesca's story, and you suspect your standards aren't shared by your in-laws, write a list of your values and beliefs. This visible tally of what matters to you will strengthen your integrity around standing up for what you believe in, and will help you treat your in-laws as you would anyone else you have put yourself out for. Make sure that your blood relation and their partner know what your ground rules are about certain things, but also make sure that you don't stick to these at the expense of everything else.

Top Tip
Go back to first principles about why you made certain
choices and check whether these still hold good for
you. This will increase your confidence about standing
up for them.

Losing touch: grandparent access

Sadly, occasionally the dynamics of the 'in-law' relationship
means that we don't have any of the leverage we might expect to
have with a blood relation.

Derek's letter

*My wife and I find ourselves in a difficult situation. Our son and
his girlfriend split up very acrimoniously and our 'daughter-in-law'
Belle has moved back to France with our only grandchild Sam.
Presumably because anything to do with our son is tainted in her
eyes, she's made it clear she wants us to leave her alone. We're
heartbroken, as Sam's a terrific little fella and we miss him dreadfully. And as much as we love our son, he hasn't been a saint in all
this, and we really feel for her too. How can we keep Sam and
Belle in our lives?*

Regards, Derek

The sad truth is that in the UK, grandparents do not have auto-
matic rights for contact with their grandchildren. And although
the family courts here recognize the valuable role grandparents
play in a child's life and very rarely refuse access, not everyone
wishes to go down the legal route.

The pain of losing contact with people we love cuts deep, especially when little remains within our control. After the trauma of the split, Belle has made choices and, for now, Derek and his wife need to respect her wishes, not least because an alternative course of action might push her and Sam further away.

The good news is that by following Belle's wishes, Derek and his wife will be demonstrating that they're listening to their son's former girlfriend, which is a fundamental kindness. After all, we all crave being heard. Bridges have been built on less.

In practical terms, Derek and his wife need to acknowledge their great sadness at this situation and mourn what is hoped will be a temporary loss. They need to take time to be kind to themselves and each other, and look for new ways to fill the gaps that Belle and Sam have left behind.

We also draft a letter to Belle and Sam in which Derek and his wife simply express their sadness about the situation and their sympathy for Belle, mentioning nothing about further meetings. Sam is nearly seven so it's appropriate that Derek and his wife remember birthdays and Christmases, which they both really want to continue doing, by sending presents and cards.

Showing respect

If you find yourself in Derek's situation, and you're faced with losing touch with someone you adore, take the time to acknowledge your own sadness and be kind to yourself as if you were grieving.

By all means, make contact because you want to, but do this because you want to make the gesture. Such gestures must be given in this spirit of generosity, and not with a view to getting anything (a card, a call, a reunion) back. In making such selfless gestures, you protect yourself from the disappointment you might feel if your hopes for something more are not met. By letting go of the hope that you'll get something specific back, you give freely of yourself, your time, your money, or your emotions while at the same time not giving a third party the power to make you feel fulfilled or complete.

Top Tip
Despite your pain, show kind respect for the wishes of your 'in-law'.

Being the carer

As we all get to live longer, we can often find that our exposure to our in-laws increases.

Davina's letter

When my mother-in-law died, it was clear from conversations in the wider family that people expected my husband Mark and me to invite his father to live with us because we have the larger house and we lived closer to him, so the move could be less disruptive. In my view my husband didn't stand up enough for us and so my father-in-law moved in. I work from home and Mark travels away on business frequently so I'm the main carer to a man I don't like. He's critical of the world, dislikes my teenage children doing their teenage thing, and generally gives off bad vibes. I used to see my home as a sanctuary but his arrival has spoiled all that. I'm at the end of my tether.

Regards, Davina

Being a carer is hard, exhausting, often thankless work. Whatever goodwill has been gained within the wider family by taking on the role, this can be heavily outweighed by resentment and home-life difficulties. Davina feels her home has been spoiled by her father-in-law's ongoing presence, and she also tells me her career has suffered. Being someone's carer means we often overlook not only the needs of loved ones but also our own needs. Davina's priority, as well as focusing on her children and her marriage, must be to reclaim her safe space and her self-worth.

Some would say that caring for elderly relatives is part of the 'duty call', the obligations of marrying into another family. Or, that we can take the moral temperature of a society by how it embraces its elderly. But within families there must be boundaries, if we are not to be overwhelmed by the needs of others. Davina feels bounced into a corner and her resentment stems from this feeling of impotence. Many people in Davina's situation speak of losing their identity. *Always saying 'yes' to people crushes our identity.*

Davina works with me on her feelings around her husband who, in her view, didn't stand up to other family members when they were petitioning that she and he should be the carers. She talks to him about getting her life back. She outlines for him the research she has done into off-site offices she might rent so that she can have uninterrupted peace for her career at certain times of the week. This will also result in needing to pay for a carer to come in on those days. When her husband complains about the cost, Davina explains that some of her husband's relatives must chip in financially. At the moment, Davina and her husband are saving the rest of the family a fortune in care-home bills. Sensibly, she has drawn up the costings.

She also timetables one evening a week for a salsa dance class and one evening a week to go out for a pizza with the children. Again, the father-in-law will need care for these times, or maybe Davina's husband would be prepared to take over on those nights? This is the moment when Davina's soft-hearted (my profession would say 'people-pleasing') husband is confronted with the true financial and emotional and temporal cost of having his father live with them, something his job has previously prevented him from seeing.

In this discussion Davina makes it clear to him, pleasantly yet assertively, that other family members need to pull their weight, in terms of time and money. This is her own boundary and for her own sanity it's appropriate that she defines it.

Boundary setting

If you find yourself in a carer situation like Davina's, shake off your pride and squash your dread of asking others for help. People like to feel useful and are often flattered to be asked. With all of us living longer, perhaps you can consider setting up grown-up versions of the Baby Sitting Circles my mother started in our village, but for elderly relatives. The added bonus of this scenario is that your elderly in-law gets new energy from the person looking after them for the evening, and this could also be a way for teenagers to earn pocket money while having exposure to old age, which would be no bad thing.

Also accept that you might not get thanks from the person you're looking after. But talk to your partner or other family members to ensure that some gratitude comes your way from them, for all your efforts.

Top Tip

Set your boundaries about workload and enjoying the other relationships in your life. These may have to be set within your marriage as much as to people outside it. In this way, you'll give yourself permission to reclaim your safe space and your self-worth.

The need for healthy separation

The main difficulty with relating to in-laws is that parents love their children unconditionally, whereas the child's partner is a constant reminder that the parent/child relationship has moved on. In an ideal world, both members of a couple will have separated healthily from their parents. Sadly, some partners, without realizing it, hope their spouse will do the separating for them. The in-law can then be blamed for upsetting the parents, while the biological son or daughter can remain 'the good child' for not being seen to choose wife/husband over mother/father.

Burying heads in the sand is not the answer. Problems with the in-laws have the potential to destroy marriages. The key is to define and set appropriate boundaries from the very beginning, which is about *taking responsibility for how we allow others to treat us.*

A survivor's guide – for the senior generation

As a survival guide, in-laws of the 'senior' generation must tread carefully and not expect to set the rules. They need to recognize the natural, necessary shift of their child away from the orbit of the parents towards a married unit or couple. Playing favourites is unacceptable, just as is ignoring or rubbishing the partner of one's child. It's natural and appropriate for a spouse to love and feel loyalty towards parents, but the 'senior' generation must accept that the primary loyalty must now be the marriage or relationship. And for the children of the in-laws, it's important to remember that we can still love our parents while disapproving of their behaviour.

A survivor's guide – for the junior generation

For the 'junior' generation, be gracious in the face of the envy of parents-in-law but remain strong and don't be afraid to stand up to disturbed behaviour aimed at you or your children. If a wife has a problem with her mother-in-law, the husband must step in and help fix it; and similarly, if a husband has difficulties with his in-laws, his wife needs to step in. It's the person with the primary relationship (the son or daughter, not the in-law) that needs to be the primary messenger; although if the in-law insists on rubbishing the message as coming only from the son-/daughter-in-law, then the couple must present a united front.

Above all, set firm boundaries from the very beginning and recognize that, especially if children come along, it is appropriate to focus on yourselves instead of being drained by in-law disturbance or overwhelmed by their needs and emotions.

And to both sides, hold on to the hope that things can improve.

CHAPTER 7
Children

Our relationships with our children have the potential to give us joy and reward, far outweighing the years of chronic sleep deprivation, the spinach thrown at the walls, the teenage sulks, and our anxieties when they eventually flee the nest. Yet our children can also hurt us beyond measure, slipping a knife through the heart with every casual neglect of our rules or our existence. The end goal is perhaps nothing more than to hope for an enjoyable relationship as adults with our own flesh and blood.

In the old days, children were to be seen and not heard. In fact, the whole notion of childhood, it is argued, is simply a seventeenth-century construct during which time liberal thinkers suggested that children were given a period of 'sanctuary' before being exposed to the hardships (i.e. employment) of adult existence. Even today, some communities in the world still lack this clear distinction between children and adults, sending children out to work as soon as they can walk, and looking to marry off offspring just before puberty.

In the West, parenting has become exceptionally child-focused. And since society is increasingly psychologically savvy, we're conscious that some of the old methods, of detachment and harsh discipline, can be counter-productive. And yet there's another school of thought that suggests that it is possible to do too much for our little darlings, raising a whole generation of narcissists who believe that the world revolves around them and who lack the resources and emotional resilience to function adequately as adults. No wonder parents feel under so much pressure to get it right.

Popularity

One issue that all parents agonize over is whether their offspring have friends.

Tania's letter

My little girl Natalie is six. Although she seems content at home, her school reports say she prefers to play on her own and doesn't have a best friend. At her school there's a rule that for birthday parties the whole class must be invited, so she does go to other girls' houses. But when I suggest holding a party or a sleepover at our house (saying we could bake cakes; she loves to help me bake cakes), she refuses to talk about it. Should I be worried or will she just grow out of the shyness?

Regards, Tania

The first thing Tania needs to assess is the quality of Natalie's shyness. Is Natalie's style to do with being at peace with herself or is she stressed or angry about something.

Open communication is the key to all relationships, so I suggest that Tania talks gently to Natalie, first about school. Maybe she's finding the scale of school overwhelming, with the number of pupils or the mass catering at lunchtimes or the size of the playground. Over time Tania can build up a picture of the things Natalie does and doesn't like about school, to see if there's anything or anyone unsettling her. Bullying can't be ruled out, so the line of questioning must be warm and gentle and casual to enable Natalie to open up about anything that's making her feel uncomfortable.

Tania and I also want the teachers to help strengthen Natalie's confidence at school. Giving a child tasks to do in class can boost morale. But other children hate to be thought a teacher's pet when they're chosen to do something, so they 'act out' their reluctance by retreating further into shyness or becoming disruptive in class. So the methods to draw Natalie out must be subtle and tailored specifically to her.

There's also another dimension to this – Natalie's home. This might be more tricky for Tania and Natalie to talk about. Some children get very protective of home, reluctant to allow the outside world to intrude. Some shy people can feel so at peace with their world they can't see the point in letting others in. Other shy types are embarrassed by home or the family members there, and are acutely alert to external judgement or approval from peers. Tania thinks this might be another thing to talk to the teachers about, to see if they can devise lessons whereby people write about home to see what Natalie might be thinking.

But I'm also conscious that Natalie is only six. She's only been at her new school two terms. Different children take to new situations in different ways, so while it's always worth having preliminary conversations about how things are going, it's also important to be patient, to allow a child's social confidence to blossom naturally. In families in particular, I'm against using labels, as it often becomes an unhelpful rather than a helpful self-fulfilling prophecy. To only talk about Natalie as 'shy' is to put her in a box that she might not know how to escape from, even if she wants to.

Above all, I want Tania to focus also on her own experience of Natalie. To treasure the child who appears content at home, who loves to help Tania bake cakes but who also enjoys the odd rough and tumble game with the males in the family. What does it mean for Tania that one of her children might be shy? Was she shy as a child and did she blossom later? Or were other family members on her or her husband's side shy?

I'm also conscious that Tania describes Natalie as her 'little girl'. Maybe there's a part of Tania that needs to keep Natalie as 'small' and unthreatening and more of a home-bunny. Tania may be more nervous than she realizes that one day Natalie will be brave and confident enough to flee the nest.

When we explore this, Tania starts weeping, recognizing that a part of her dreads the day that her children won't need her any more. Without realizing it, Tania is conflicted: she wants to help Natalie conquer her shyness but can see how the shy Natalie is less likely to 'abandon' her. Now that this conflict in Tania is conscious, Tania can make a conscious effort to concentrate on making sure that Natalie is fulfilled and content.

Exploring shyness

If Tania's story resonates for you, and you have a child who is shy at home or school, avoid labelling your child negatively. Understand that being shy is about a personality type, not about something being 'wrong'. Some people never stop being shy, but many of them still exude a quiet self-confidence that is attractive to be around. They make good listeners, and once they make friends they often do so for life. Instead, discuss home and school gently with your child, to find out if something is troubling them. But also be aware of your own unconscious motives, in case it suits you to have a clingy or shy child.

Top Tip
Shyness can mean many things, so it's important to identify what type of shyness your child is exhibiting. For example, is your child self-contained and at peace with the world or are they anxious or angry about something. This way you can determine whether it's something you need to help them address or whether it's just their nature.

Bullying

Bullying is not a new phenomenon but, with the rise of social media and the number of children who have access to mobile phones and computers, parents need to be ever more vigilant for the ways in which bullying can be perpetrated.

Jackie's letter

My husband and I overheard Josh, our ten-year-old, talking in another room to some of his friends about horrible messages to send to another boy, about the way he walks and what he looks like. I know the boy in question and he has cerebral palsy, so I'm horrified my son thinks it's okay to tease this poor child for his disability. I say tease, but deep down I know it's bullying, plain and simple. My son is turning into a bully. My husband's furious and wants to throw away Josh's mobile phone, but I think we need to change his behaviour. What do you think?

Regards, Jackie

We humans are hugely imitative creatures. We learn about the world, and how to function in it, by copying others. The jury's still out for most of us regarding the argument about child development, whether nature or nurture plays the bigger part – I think it's a bit of both, depending on the child in question. This means that Josh will have picked up the bullying tactics from somewhere – his friends, the television, movies or game consuls.

Jackie and her husband need to become the corrective influence, demonstrating an anti-bullying stance. We three role-play conversations she or her husband can have with Josh about what bullying means and why it's always unacceptable. Storylines in soap operas or movies can be great for sparking casual-sounding conversations about crucial topics with the kids in our lives. From such conversations Josh can learn about bullying, its impact on people, and why it must be stopped at every turn.

Since it's the parental lot to correct and reprimand for unacceptable behaviour, we also talk about her husband's impulse to throw Josh's phone away. Both agree they want to take a firm line. They tell Josh they'll stop his privileges (pocket money, mobile phone) if they catch him bullying, or planning to bully anyone again.

It's also important that they applaud Josh when he does kindly or empathic things for others, including his parents and other family members. School staff can be co-opted into this process. Jackie asks to be alerted if the teachers feel her son is bullying others. She also talks to the mums of the boys involved to see what they've noticed about their sons' behaviours.

But of course no-one can supervise Josh or his friends all the time. The ideal is for Jackie to model for Josh a no-tolerance approach to bullying that he can then begin to copy himself.

Curbing bullying

If Jackie's situation echoes yours and you worry your child is a bully, firmly model for your child a non-bullying attitude. After all, developing respect towards others begins at home. Also pay attention to your relationships at home to check that there's no subtle bullying going on between siblings or between you as parents. Also use stories in the media or in current affairs to initiate discussions about why bullying is never acceptable.

Top Tip
Praise and sometimes reward your child when they do kindly things, such as washing-up, reading to siblings, or when they show spontaneous warmth towards others.

Tough love

The major issue in parent/child relationships is the shifting power dynamic. At birth the grown-ups hold the majority of the cards, but very quickly it becomes a relationship where accommodation and negotiation of positions must take place. Developmental milestones affect parent/child relationships, and the skill of parenting is to manage adequately the emotions of the child while retaining the integrity, self-esteem, and sense of personal space of the adult.

Karen's letter

I'm a single mum and I'm struggling to get my son Noah to respect me. He's always telling me I'm an awful mum, but that his dad is amazing. I share custody with my ex, Noah's dad, and I've never bad-mouthed him, even though he went off with someone else. But now Noah is twelve he's been hanging around with a bad gang from our estate. My ex says I need to be more assertive. But Noah takes no notice when I try to tell him off. He says he hates me and to be honest, even though I love him as my son, I think I hate him too. But this just makes me feel guilty so I end up giving in. What can I do?

Regards, Karen

Noah is indulging in 'splitting', pretending that one parent is 'all good' and the other parent 'all bad'. Noah is playing one parent off against the other, and gaining the upper hand. Karen demonstrates the classic human conflict that we often hate the people we love. This happens especially in childhood, when the good mummy who kisses us goodnight is also the bad mummy who makes us share our toys.

Karen struggles with her son's hatred of her. As grown-ups we can see that infant rage is childlike and harmless. But when our kids get older, their attacks start to feel accurate and personal. They work out what wounds us and even their more casual attacks often go to the heart of our own secret insecurities. As a single mum left additionally vulnerable after her ex's infidelity, Noah's accusation that Karen is a bad mum (and therefore a bad person) strikes a painful chord.

A crucial stage in childhood development is for a child to see a parent as both 'good' and 'bad'. Karen isn't bad in trying to take a tough line with her son, she's doing what any good parent would do. But instead of wanting Noah to like her, Karen's focus must be on ignoring her guilt and getting him to respect her.

Karen needs to take control of her emotions first before addressing the relationship with Noah. My suggestion to Karen is to work on improving her self-respect. This will make her a stronger individual with more self-confidence, which will make her better able to tolerate those moments when she hates her son. A personal attack on us is like Velcro: it can only stick if we possess a similar piece of Velcro, or doubt about our Self. If Noah sees that his accusations *no longer* wind Karen up, he'll soon drop them.

Out of Karen's increased self-respect will come the confidence to withstand Noah's hateful impulses. It's vital that children of all ages learn that parents can tolerate being hated. If we don't experience that sense, then we become terrified that our attacks on our parents will damage them. Our guilt from this terror becomes intolerable.

What Karen needs to abandon is her desire that Noah must like her. Once she lets go of this desire (a desire which can be met by other people in her life, such as her friends and maybe, one day, a new partner), she'll find it easier to take a tougher line with Noah, because it won't matter that he hates her for doing so. By being assertive with Noah while at the same time showing her commitment to him and his wellbeing, Noah will develop respect for Karen. Change will not happen over night and in the very darkest moments it can feel like a thankless task, but that's the essence of parenting. If your children end up liking you, that's a wonderful bonus.

Disciplining children

If Karen's story resonates for you, and you're struggling to discipline your child, keep in mind that it's unhelpful to think children must like their parents. Parenting isn't about being your child's best friend. Healthy parenting is about rules and boundaries and loving your children unconditionally. It's about recognizing that children are small balls of unruly impulses, such as wanting to eat sweets before meals, impulses that you must curb and frustrate if kids are to learn about self-control and delayed gratification and respect for the self and others. This is why your child seems to hate you.

The key is to work on your self-respect by reminding yourself of your talents and achievements, and to have other people in your life who like you. This way you'll be able to withstand their hateful impulses and concentrate on being a firm yet loving parent.

Top Tip
Be consistent with your child, so they know where they stand with regard to household rules and discipline. If, for example, you want them to have done something (laying the table, say) 'by the count of three', stick to that limit. It might feel like Groundhog Day but over time, your child will learn that you mean what you say. This will make them feel less confused around you, which will cause you less stress.

Early influences

We bring our life history to the role of parenting, which can affect our relationship with our children.

Katie's letter

I'm forty-one and recently my adoptive mother died. I loved her but for years I've suffered from depression about having been re-jected as a baby. Just lately I've worried that I should by now have told my kids (who are in their teens) that I'm adopted. I was told about my circumstances as part of my tenth birthday celebrations. I struggled with this bombshell information, and even now my husband is the only other person who knows. I'm not sure I'll be able to handle all the questions my kids might have, especially about not having said anything to them before. In short, I'm afraid they'll think I've lied to them by omission. I lie awake at night, wondering what to do for the best. Please help.

Regards, Katie

Katie has long struggled with the dramatic change in her identity brought about by being told she was adopted. Now, with the death of her adopted mother, feelings around identity are surfacing: will her own children think she's a liar? In both the past and the present, Katie is left feeling inadequate and unable to meet the expectations of others.

We talk about how she felt when she was originally told she was adopted. As much as she loved her adopted parents she felt over-whelmed by hurt and sadness, and rage at having been abandoned. Although she hasn't even told her husband this, it also privately upset her that her parents had somehow tainted her tenth birthday with this news, although as an adult she recognizes that this news might have unsettled her whenever it had been revealed.

It's interesting to note that her own children, fifteen-year-old twins, a boy and a girl, are now much older than Katie was when she was given the news. For years she's held off telling them. Possibly she's been trying to protect them from news that upset her as a child. Or possibly she's tried to suppress the knowledge as a form of denial, so that her children can live in what she imagines is blissful ignorance, to compensate for when her own bliss was ruptured in childhood.

She also worries she won't be able to handle their questions and that they'll accuse her of lying to them all these years. My suggestion to Katie is that this is a double echo from the past: a fear she won't be able to live up to her children's expectations, plus an ongoing yet unexpressed resentment that, aged ten, Katie felt her adopted parents had been 'lying' to her until then.

Being adopted left Katie with feelings of inadequacy and mistrust, which have contributed to her depression. It explains why she has only told her husband that she's adopted; she has never felt confident that other people in her life will understand the enormity of this information.

Although Katie's question to me is about how to handle revealing this news to her kids, it's an opportunity for Katie to process the fact that she's adopted. Katie's question is less about wondering whether her kids are old enough for this revelation, and more about feeling comfortable about certain aspects of her past.

Healing the past

If Katie's story resonates for you, examine your history to see what emotions and events affect your behaviour with your children in the present. Work out whether there are things you want to talk to them about, or whether these are things you can process on your own or by talking to a friend or with professional help.

Examine and have compassion for your feelings about what happened to you, and look to strengthen your sense of self, so that you can come to terms with what happened in your past.

Top Tip
Remember that your children aren't you, and may react to information differently to how you did. Remember, too, that children are fabulously self-centred and often aren't that interested in things that happened in their own family before they arrived.

The teenage brain

When parenting teenagers, the world suddenly seems to be riddled with wild hormones and abrupt changes in behavioural direction.

Melissa's letter

Our son Matthew is just seventeen. Last year he asked me if his girlfriend at the time could stay over. At the risk of sounding prudish, my husband and I said 'no'. I gather they broke up a few months ago and Matthew joined the local cricket and hockey teams, which I thought was healthy. Unfortunately, it turns out that he's the youngest in the teams and on Saturday nights he now gets very drunk with the older men at the club. When I now hear him talking about women it's with contempt, once even criticizing me for wearing a dress above the knee (I am not yet forty-three.). I feel I've lost my son. Should my husband and I be worried by this change in him?

Regards, Melissa

Initially Melissa was pleased that, at sixteen, Matthew felt he had a good enough relationship with her to ask about having a girlfriend over. She said 'no', but now she's torturing herself that she has somehow given the impression that sex is wrong, or that girls who want sex at sixteen are sluts or some variation on this theme.

We work on Melissa acquiring compassion for the choice she made back then. Parenting is largely about boundary control and delaying gratification so that kids can learn healthy self-control. So, whether the world at large agrees with her or not, one of Melissa's values is to believe that sixteen was too young for her son to be having sex.

Talking to our children about sex is complicated but it can be immensely rewarding. It's about demonstrating trust and feeling trusted. And for the grown-ups, it's about conveying core values to our children about love, intimacy, and safety in a loving, non-rejecting way. Even though our late teen children might come across as swaggering adults, deep down they're still vulnerable and will still benefit from parental support.

The tricky thing about such conversations is that they're often held at a time when adolescents are undergoing radical change. Current research shows that adolescents go through tremendous brain development. Some of these changes take place in the very part of the brain that controls planning and impulse control and reasoning. We as adults get immensely frustrated at the new passions embraced by adolescents, the risk-taking and the apparent neglect of reason, but this is partly due to changes in the brain which have to happen and which adolescents can't control, even if they wanted to.

As a result, adolescence is a time of great experimentation. Teenagers are starting to healthily separate from their parents and perhaps form friendships with other adults who will influence then differently, such as colleagues at work or tutors at university or, as with Matthew, fellow members of his local sports teams.

Some of this separation happens by 'rejecting' the values and codes the parents represent. It may involve taking up political or social causes, dressing provocatively, smoking, taking drugs, having under-age sex, getting blind drunk, and many other behaviours most adults regard as upsetting or dangerous or ridiculous or illegal.

Let's be clear: parents are behaving entirely appropriately in trying to steer their kids away from harmful activities. But the context for all this, just so we know what we're dealing with, is that, overall, this journey away from the parents is *necessary* for strengthening a person's identity and sense of self. In other words, it's appropriate. And on some level this makes it less personal.

What Melissa's son Matthew is demonstrating is that the teenage years are also very much about finding peer approval and acceptance. Socially he is now hanging around with older, more sexually experienced men and he has also perhaps recently ended an intimate, probably sexual relationship. Melissa and I discuss how she might broach this subject, to talk in general about sex and attitudes to women, again using stories in the news or on the Internet as well as storylines in soaps to generate casual conversation, to show that sex is not a taboo topic as far as Melissa is concerned. We discuss how it made her feel when Matthew criticized her dress sense. It seems to her that maybe Matthew was angry at his ex-girlfriend and wanted to take this out on the nearest woman in his life.

She role-plays with me talking to him about the subject of women and what they wear and how he feels about women in general. But we also want to ensure that Melissa doesn't come across as nosey and intrusive about his life. Teenagers must have their privacy respected, if they're to grow up feeling respected. Men in particular who have nosey or controlling mothers can feel hemmed in and defensive around women. This in turn can lead to anger towards women in later life.

Finding peer acceptance might also mean that Matthew is, without realizing it, adopting or exaggerating some of the attitudes displayed by his sports club peers, the older men at the cricket and hockey clubs, to feel he belongs or to come across as more macho than he truly feels. His comments about women could also be masking anxiety in front of men who he imagines must be more sexually experienced.

Understanding what may be going on for her son is helpful for Melissa and her husband. It helps them place Matthew's behaviour in both an evolutionary and a personal context.

Of course, since we're imitative creatures, Melissa and her husband agree to monitor their own behaviour to see whether their interaction could give rise to Matthew believing that it's all right to treat women with contempt. Even the way parents thank each other (or not) for the daily tasks of providing supper or driving, or compliment each other (or not) on how they are looking or for something they have done, will influence our children in their relationships with future loved ones. Saying 'I don't like to hear women denigrated' means that Melissa vocalizes in a non-judgemental way her own moral code, instead of criticizing her son. It's a subtle difference, but one that makes teenagers feel less attacked.

Striking a balance

If Melissa's story resonates for you, and you're struggling with the changes exhibited by your teenager, you need to strike a balance between protecting your child by expressing your core values and boundaries, and giving them the freedom to experiment with who they are or who they want to become. And take comfort from the fact that due to the brain developments mentioned above, some of your child's more extreme attitudes may settle back down naturally once their brain has fully matured.

Since this can be an immensely overwhelming and hormone-driven time for teenagers, when they're trying to work out who they are, your consistent love and support is valuable, even if your child takes decades to thank you for it.

Top Tip
Develop ways of withstanding your child's apparent rejection of you, by recognizing that this is all part of a necessary shift away from parental control, while at the same time remaining true to your core ideals.

Empty nest syndrome

After all the dramas of childhood, there comes a time when we're faced with the prospect of the kids leaving home, if not for good, then for the first time.

Fiona's letter

Barney, my youngest son of three, is off travelling to Asia in September before starting college and already I'm terrified. I've found myself getting breathless when out in the town, worrying he won't be safe. He was seriously ill as a child with an eye condition that at one time looked as though it would rob him of his sight, but he came through all that, and studied hard, so this place at college is a symbol of all his courage and determination. I'm so proud. And yet I don't want him to go. Of course I haven't dared mention any of this to my husband; he'd just think I'm a

*daft old brush. But there are days when I don't know how I'll
survive his going.*

Regards, Fiona

Fiona is suffering from 'separation anxiety', which is very common
in mother/child relationships. If you've ever watched toddlers
trotting off happily for their first day of school while the mothers
stride tearfully back down the street you'll recognize the sense of
loss that some can experience at these normal developmental
milestones.

Yet at the same time, we recognize that the parenting ideal is to
raise our kids in such a secure and loving way that when they do
eventually leave us, they grab the world with both hands and lead
fulfilling lives of their own. Fiona's husband might simply point
out, hopefully less bluntly than me, that this is how it's meant to
be. Even so, it can be a huge knock to our equilibrium to be faced
with the reality that we are now, and probably for years to come,
surplus to requirements.

Influencing Fiona's anxieties is the fact that Barney is her
youngest. When the other two sons went off to work and college
there was always the knowledge in the back of her mind that, like
Tania with her shy daughter Natalie, there was still Barney back
home. And now Barney is leaving too. This moment isn't simply
mobilizing the sense of loss we often experience when a child
leaves home, this last child leaving is the end of a mothering era,
a potent symbol of the potential for redundancy.

Barney's childhood illness is of course contributing to Fiona's
worries. We all worry about our children, but if there has ever
been major illness in the mix, there often remains that nagging
sense that bad things might happen again. Who wouldn't have a
twinge of doubt, of fear, of panic in Fiona's shoes?

The mistake is to behave in such a way that Barney suspects he
doesn't have permission to leave home, that somehow his mother

won't survive without him. There are some families where this message is unconsciously conveyed, where one child, even when an adult, spends a disproportionate amount of time 'back home', who perhaps moves only to the next street, or who turns down job offers or even relationships as a way of keeping those apron strings intact.

Fiona needs to address the intrusive thoughts in her head that Barney will be unsafe overseas. With Facebook and phones it's so much easier to keep in touch with offspring than it was a generation ago, when I announced to my appalled parents at the age of eighteen that I would be going to Peru without knowing a word of Spanish. The options of quick and safe money transfers can also now soothe the fretting minds of parents who worry that their children will get themselves into tricky situations requiring financial assistance thousands of miles away.

Fiona and I discuss who else she can confide in at this time, to receive empathy from others going through the same experience, perhaps other mums with children off to new jobs or college or travelling. And also to have open communication with her husband, reminiscing but also planning for the new life they have ahead of them.

Embracing the future

If Fiona's story echoes yours, and you're dreading your child leaving the nest, bear in mind that by experiencing real-life situations and having (and surviving) knock-backs, your kids can grow and learn and develop. Feel proud that you've raised a child to the best of your ability and acknowledge that a lengthy era is coming to an end. Take time perhaps to mourn that end, and then set about reclaiming your life, filling it with exciting new projects and people.

If you're single, this can be the first time in a long while when you feel as though this time can be just for you, perhaps to think for the first time about entering a new relationship, which can be a daunting yet exciting challenge. If you're in a couple, you now have opportunities to re-connect as a couple and not be so child-centric, to deepen the relationship as friends as much as co-parents.

Whatever your situation, more activities means less time to dwell on the absence. Healthy separation leads to confidence on both sides of the parent/child equation, and therefore there's a greater chance that future reunions will be valued more, on both sides.

Top Tip
Practise smiling enthusiastically at all the plans, while grieving only in private. Finding other mothers in this situation, online or in your area, can provide you with support as you enter this new phase of being a parent.

Children and divorce

Sometimes our relationships with our children are affected by events within the family, such as infidelity or divorce.

Nick's letter

After years of difficult relations, my wife and I are divorcing. I was unfaithful a couple of times, and now my wife has had enough. We have two beautiful children, aged nearly fifteen and eleven, who I'm sure will be relieved their parents are no longer fighting. But at the moment, even though I'm worried about all the legal and financial aspects of the impending divorce, I'm also conscious that my kids are bound to be affected by the news when we tell them. Can you give me any pointers as to how to handle my relationship with my children at this time and perhaps in the near future?

Regards, Nick

Nick is right to acknowledge that this imminent moment of clarity, when the divorce is announced, will affect *everyone* emotionally – not just the children. Sometimes the biggest struggle for parents is to continue to be emotionally available to their children at the very time when they're feeling overwhelmed and emotionally depleted.

The sad fact is that sometimes divorce is so painful that family members don't know how to show their pain, or don't know if they have permission to show the pain. Nick and his wife need to be alert to the ways in which children 'act out' their emotional distress. For example, infants may 'act out' their emotions by destroying toys, because they lack verbal or cognitive skills; school children may feel obliged to side with one parent or the other, whereas teenagers can become cynical about relationships or feel the need to rush into relationships of their own for security. And if some children appear to be unfazed by it all, deep down it could all be a front, an attempt to try to protect the precious adults from even more emotion. Nick and his wife need to be available to their children when they want to talk or express their emotion.

At the same time, children faced with this new reality can gain strength from seeing their parents relating in a calm and agreeable manner. Nick and his wife are planning to speak to the children as a couple, to show a united front. However, Nick is conscious that his infidelities have been the trigger for the marital breakdown. The context of many divorces can make parental relations incredibly strained, if not openly hostile. It can take enormous amounts of self-control not to bad-mouth the partner who has been unfaithful, or who has gambled away the savings, who is violent or racist or demonstrates other unacceptable behaviour.

Still, children can learn an incredibly valuable lesson for their future intimate relationships if they see their parents behaving in a mature, cooperative fashion and not blaming the other party – even when inside the adults are screaming with pain.

This typical inner pain is something people in Nick's situation must address. Good self-care is vital. Nick joked that he could kip down on a mate's sofa for a few weeks, and I'm all for humour to see us through life's painful transitions. But to maintain good relations with our children in the post-divorce world, we must maintain good self-care. We must take our sleep and eating patterns immensely seriously, and find ways to process the emotional pain. We can't be strong for our kids if we don't look after ourselves.

Post-divorce openness

In 2010, there were 104,364 children in England and Wales under the age of sixteen when their parents divorced that year,[1] which just shows how many children are affected by this process. If Nick's story echoes yours, and you're about to or have announced a divorce from your partner, accept that your children could have many questions for weeks or months to come about this highly unsettling development. At the same time, derive strength from the fact that children are resilient creatures. Your children have the capacity to adjust and thrive in the brave new world, post-divorce.

Keep your lines of communication open, and work hard to relate to your partner in a calm and agreeable manner in front of your children. Your children will experience different, age-related, insecurities at different times. The world they know, the security they took for granted, has evaporated. This will be absolutely terrifying, especially if your children are unable to articulate their feelings adequately yet. Questions may arise at the time of being told about the divorce but, as the reality sinks in, as your children process this news in their own way, they may formulate different questions later, or start to react emotionally, for which they will need your help and reassurance.

Top Tip

It's crucial to take care of yourself emotionally and physically so you can be fully available to your children at this exhausting time, such as eating and sleeping properly, together with building a support network of friends for you to confide in and let off steam with.

Step-families

One by-product of divorce can be a new step-family.

Olivia's letter

My second husband and I have three children between us, my son and his two daughters. I'm a divorcee, Pete's a widower. We've just had a daughter of our own and Pete's girls are behaving dreadfully. They play their music really loud when Lily's sleeping and they gang up on me when Pete's at work. They yell, 'you can't tell me what to do, you're not our mother.' Pete and I want to think it's their age, because they're just hitting their teens (twelve and fourteen) but it's like they don't want to know Lily exists – which I find hurtful. How can I make things work in this step-family so that in the future my daughter can have good relations with all her siblings, and not just my son?

Regards, Olivia

In addition to the strains as well as the joys of being a mother again, Olivia is coping with two girls who are struggling to deal with their own emotional conflicts. After the trauma of losing their mother, and getting to know a new lady in their father's life, Pete's girls have now got a new rival for their father's affections – Lily. And the more people coo over how wonderful Lily is, the more Pete's daughters resent her and what she represents. They haven't chosen any aspect of the way events have panned out over the last few years. They probably feel voiceless and afraid for the future and anxious about being 'replaced'.

Even though the girls are twelve and fourteen respectively, they're still young emotionally. Their attachment to their father is still that of a child. It's possible that they also see Olivia as solely responsible for this turn of events – not in the sense that they don't yet understand how babies are conceived, but more in the sense that it's easier to blame the 'outsider', which as far as their family triangle is concerned, is Olivia.

Olivia explores with me what it means for her to raise children who get on. Olivia has a sister with whom she gets on well; when Olivia's marriage was breaking down, her sister was the person she confided in most. So for Olivia, her family template is of siblings who offer concrete emotional support. So, naturally, she longs for this for her new daughter. (Her son from her first marriage, seems chuffed with the arrival of Lily – as much as boys can be interested in a baby girl seven years younger. His overall view is that he's no longer The Baby, so Lily's arrival has been a positive for him.)

Pete's daughters are dumping their pain and resentment on Olivia, who is in the emotionally vulnerable position of nursing a new baby. Pete and Olivia must work as a team more than ever on this one, keeping the channels of communication open with the girls who, in addition to their feelings about Pete's remarriage and the arrival of Lily, are probably still grieving the death of their mother.

So at first the conversations Olivia and Pete have with the girls end up being more about their real mother. What Olivia realizes is that the more the girls resent Lily, the more she resents them for resenting Lily.

With this insight about herself, Olivia works hard at sharing her 'resentments' only with me, so that when she's with the girls she's free to be completely and authentically warm and sympathetic to them, keeping in her mind what they've lost and how young they still are. Olivia sees that what she needs to do for a time is over-compensate by being overly motherly to the girls, while paying attention to her feelings in private (in the beginning of her relationship with Pete she had resisted, as she didn't want to be accused of trying to be a 'replacement' mum). Conversations with the girls give them the chance to feel heard within the new family unit. As with all parent/child conflict, one very helpful technique is to help the child find a solution instead of always being the parent who fixes things. So the girls are given the chance to create some of the house rules, and discuss ways to compromise.

Olivia also starts being more tactful about how much time she talks about Lily, if at all, and Pete starts organizing a treat a week alone with the girls. At first Olivia was concerned to think they might be pandering to the girls, but by putting herself in the girls' shoes, she sees how much they need the reassurance from both Olivia and Pete that there is enough love to go round, even in extended or step-families. Once the girls felt more secure after the radical change of Lily's arrival, over time they became more accepting of her and warmer towards Olivia.

Becoming the step-parent

If Olivia's story resonates for you, and you're struggling with step-child resentments, with your partner set parameters about what you're capable of doing and what not. If, for example, you're nursing a new baby, you'll need extra support from your partner, friends, and family.

At the same time, acknowledge your own feelings about having to care for children who aren't yours, which may include resentment and anger. Be prepared to process this emotion away from the children.

Top Tip

Recognize that even older children can revert to childlike behaviour when rivals (you or any new babies) appear on the scene. You can't be the replacement parent your step-children have lost, but you can aim to be a strong and loving adult support to them, talking to them about their feelings and helping see why they feel the way they do.

Developing self-awareness

From his or her birth, your child is one of many 'Others' with whom you develop a relationship. And as in all relationships, how you conduct yourself often tells you as much about yourself as it does about your child.

Whatever their age, your relationships with your children require lots of thought. Examining yourself for the kind of relationships you experienced as a child is a useful tool in working out what you reject and bring to your parenting techniques. As ever, self-awareness is crucial in understanding how to manage your relationships with your children, and to recognize that these relationships too will change with time. When some women say that their daughter is their best friend, this can jar with others who feel that parents need to be parents, with all the boundary setting and rule enforcement this entails.

Yet as we age and both child and parent become adults together, the relationship can develop into one that has all the hallmarks of friendship, such as mutual respect and support and understanding for all the dramas that went before.

CHAPTER 8
Work-ships: The New Playground

In many ways, the workplace *is* the new playground. Colleagues work with us for the same company, the same family as it were, and we share (hopefully) the same goal in making the company or its product or its reputation or its balance sheet the best it can be in any given year. But at the same time, colleagues compete with us for the resources available: the peachy assignment, the promotion, the bonus pot or the corner office. And because the set up of an office can closely resemble a family in terms of hierarchy, unresolved patterns and conflicts from childhood can resurface.

Needy colleagues

A work environment can be made up of a range of personalities. There's the cool crowd, the alpha males and females, the wreckers, the naughty children – and the panickers.

Millie's letter

In general I like my job, but whenever I need to leave the office, either for a work commitment or – heaven forbid – go on holiday, my boss smothers me with questions and requests. By the end of the encounter I'm either a) late or b) stressed. And if this happens before I go on holiday, I end up spending my entire trip feeling guilty. Why does he do this and how can I stop getting caught up in this game?

Regards, Millie

When Millie is due to leave the office appropriately, her boss panics and becomes very needy. He's like a child suffering separation anxiety. Children fear abandonment, especially when they're young. At this age, they lack the understanding that people or objects still exist even when they can't be seen. So when they first start school, for example, it takes them a while to trust that mummy is coming back each day to collect them.

Something in Millie's boss makes him feel insecure when Millie is about to go out of sight, whether it's for a meeting out of the office or on holiday. It's appropriate to want to know that contingency plans are in place, to know that projects are under control or will be competently handled in Millie's absence. But to pile on the pressure so that an employee feels guilty for doing their job or taking a holiday is not appropriate. Sadly, Millie gets caught up in seeing things from his perspective, so her absences make her feel guilty, as though she's genuinely done something wrong.

In working out how to deal with the frustration, I ask Millie to think about why this scenario makes her feel, for example, guilty rather than angry – or stressed rather than dismissive. Because as I've said before, the bumps in the road in our relationships will always say as much about *us* as they do about The Other. Millie recognizes that she has a fear of being rejected, in the form of being fired. This is what drives her to be so conscientious at work. Her guilt and stress are actually closer to buried anger. Anger that her boss's behaviour gives the impression that he doesn't trust her to do a thorough handover or to have thought through all the possibilities that might occur in her absence.

She also feels angry that she's made to feel that her holidays are a dreadful inconvenience. What she deserves is a boss who appreciates her hard work and who recognizes that holidays are justified. Or who sees that meetings off-site or presentations to clients are as important to her job as her presence in the office. Someone, in other words, who is reasonable.

And yet she fears her own anger. It unsettles her that if she were to show her true feelings, her anger or irritation, her boss might be angry back. She might even jeopardize her job. This makes her suppress those feelings and turn them onto herself in the form of guilt.

Millie now knows where her emotions are coming from. And although we can't see into the mind of her boss, Millie is gracious enough to say that apart from his pre-absence meltdowns, she and he have a good working relationship. So the next stage is to draw up plans to deal with future panicky questions and obstacles. The key is to deal with her boss rather as a parent deals with a child, trying to encourage them to separate healthily. Even though her imminent absence makes her boss anxious, she is still going to go (to the meeting/on holiday), but at the same time she'll be reassuring.

Setting boundaries

If Millie's story echoes yours and you have a panicking colleague, take control of the situation and book time to see them *ahead of your absence*. Brief them on the cover arrangements you've put in place while away and find out if they have any questions or concerns. This means pro-actively taking control not just of the conversation but also its timing.

With regard to holidays, make sure to talk about the forthcoming break in neutral terms, without apology. This means that you're acknowledging that taking a holiday is appropriate, and also reminds your colleague not to try and blur the boundary with a request to remain in phone or email contact while you're away.

At the same time, reassure colleagues that your absence from the workplace will see you return re-energized.

Top Tip
Manage your colleague firmly but with reassurance. Also ask yourself whether your own emotions or mood are affected by their behaviour, to see whether this relationship has echoes in your past. If it does, work on any unresolved issues from home so that you don't find yourself re-enacting childhood dramas in the office.

The in-crowd

If we work in a large office or department, there may be dozens of characters we have to interact with. Yet most groups, no matter their size, have an in-crowd.

Tara's letter

I work in a male-dominated environment and on a daily basis know I perform as well as if not better than the men. But when it comes to down-time and socializing after work, I'm excluded from the Alpha gang, not because I'm female – my colleagues would love it if I came along – but because I don't like drinking ten pints of beer and going to lap-dancing clubs. I've tried not caring but I'm aware I miss out on informal conversations about deals, appraisals and the general gossip that keeps me in the loop. Any ideas what to do?

Regards, Tara

The problem with trying to become part of a group is that groups develop subtle codes to keep out 'undesirables'. In the workplace, such codes can be about anything, from schooling to training, gender to personality. Most organizations spawn a more elite group within, who are generally tapped into priority information about the group or organization. For Tara it brings back memories of school and of being only half in with the in-crowd.

Tara was regarded as a bit of a swot, but she was also good at netball. So for certain times of the year when netball was played, Tara found herself part of the popular group of girls. This made her feel wanted and liked and therefore validated. But because her membership of this group was temporary, it also made her annoyed and resentful. Eventually, as she matured, she needed the approval of the popular girls less, but she's surprised at how quickly she reverts to the emotions of school, when 'belonging' mattered more.

Tara needs to do two things: she needs to get herself to a place where declining the invitation to go out for ten beers doesn't leave her feeling worthless or resentful. In other words, she needs to examine her insecurities around not being part of the gang. And she also needs to explore whether she can suggest or organize activities to break the imaginative tradition of the beer/lap-dance evenings.

We first draw up a list of the ways Tara can feel validated, both by herself and by others. Tara regards her salary and bonuses as validation, but also the comments made during appraisal times. She has a good relationship with the secretary and her clients. Outside work, she's proud of having run the London Marathon, and plans to participate again to see if she can beat her own time. Another thing Tara likes about herself is that she's trying to become a better cook by finding out more about the African and Caribbean vegetables on sale in her local market.

Tara suggests a couple of social events with her colleagues: ten-pin bowling, and bootcamp-style training one evening in a nearby park. Two things are revealed from these suggestions. One is that several colleagues privately thank Tara for getting them out of having to sink ten pints on a weeknight. The power of the group has been that no-one wanted to raise their head above the parapet and confess they're bored with or disapprove of that form of socializing.

The other is that the bootcamp idea, far from being a one-off, becomes a regular once-a-week event, which Tara is at the heart of. After training, many of the group still repair to the pub, but there's now less stigma about not drinking alcohol, and Tara is more comfortable attending. By looking both at herself and at her environment, and being pleasantly assertive and pro-active, Tara has made her work-ship culture work for her.

Taking control

If Tara's story sounds familiar, and you have a powerful in-crowd in your firm, examine your feelings about being in or out of it. Not everyone wants to be part of the elite group (some people prefer to remain outsiders, as observers, seeing which way the wind blows), but the existence of this group and our inclusion or exclusion will always bring up something for each of us.

Dream up ways to pro-actively assert yourself to co-exist with the in-crowd on your terms, such as suggesting social events or, within work, suggesting new ways to tackle projects. Remember that simply doing your job well can be a route to inclusion, if inclusion is important for you.

Top Tip
Think about the triggers in your office for making you feel the way you do, and validate yourself by identifying what makes you feel good, both at work and in your down-time.

Mental health in the workplace

It is sometimes hard to make the culture work for us when the issue is mental health.

Ricky's letter

I was diagnosed as bi-polar when I was nineteen, but apart from a few members of my family, I haven't told anyone. I didn't, for example, tell my company when I was interviewed and I've now been here four years. Because of the economic climate, there's now quite a tense atmosphere at work, and I worry that my boss is watching me more carefully, with every doctor's appointment I take. This is making me take work home and work well into the night, which aggravates my bi-polar. I don't know whether to reveal my illness to my boss, or whether coming clean will put me in the firing line for having kept things secret until now.

Regards, Ricky

Ricky's refusal to be defined by his mental illness is inspiring. As Nicky Morgan MP said in a debate in the House of Commons in June 2012, 'we all have mental health, it's just some people's is better than others.'

And yet, sadly, a huge amount of work still needs to be done to address the stigma of mental illness in the workplace. In 2011, the mental health charity MIND presented evidence to show that employees who admit at work to mental health concerns, fear being sacked or squeezed out of their jobs. Not every employee is blessed with an enlightened boss, so Ricky's initial decision not to mention his illness, at interview or subsequently, is entirely understandable.

I ask Ricky to look at where his current stress is coming from. The current global economic uncertainties are definitely contributing to workplace anxieties up and down the country, across all industries. Yet how much are Ricky's worries to do with this climate and how much are they to do with his guilt at having kept something secret from his boss? This kind of guilt plays on our mind. We imagine others can spot our guilty feelings and, because we feel bad, we imagine such people are cross with us. So, Ricky needs to assess how likely it is that having worked successfully for the company for four years, his job is now under threat.

I suggest Ricky turns to the friends and family who *do* know about his bi-polar disorder and talks to them about his anxieties. Getting things off our chest can make them feel less toxic, more bearable. And these conversations with family members can provide practice should he decide subsequently to speak to his boss. It's much easier initiating a difficult conversation with someone when you've practised it and know exactly what you want to convey.

I also suggest Ricky thinks about striking up the odd conversation with colleagues about mental health issues when they appear in the media. With celebrities and politicians opening up about their mental health issues, storylines in soap operas, and phone-ins on radio programmes often linked to news items about mental health, it's easier than ever to talk about what MIND calls the 'Elephant in the Room'. Ricky doesn't have to disclose information about himself, but it might be a useful way to test out the reactions of others in the office to the topic of mental illness.

Working on himself, Ricky might also usefully pay attention to his self-esteem. Cutting back on working during the night will mean Ricky is not jeopardizing his own self-care.

Coming clean about mental illness

If Ricky's situation speaks to you, and you're currently wondering whether to mention a previously undisclosed mental health issue, don't panic; instead, with the help of friends, calmly assess whether you need to reveal your condition.

I'm torn, because I believe honesty in our relationships is always the best policy. Yet if there's no suggestion that your performance is in doubt, it's possible, for example, that a negative interpretation will be placed on the fact that you didn't fully disclose your health situation initially (although of course different companies have radically different policies on this).

I'd like to imagine that most bosses would be sympathetic, but remember that if, by going public about your mental illness you receive negative reactions, MIND has a brilliant legal advice line (0300 466 6463), so you can find out where you stand.

Top Tip

At all times, pay attention to your self-care. Watching out for those times when your self-esteem becomes too wrapped up in only one section of your life gives you the opportunity to re-introduce balance into your routine. Being conscientious about work is important, but not to the extent that it takes over your life.

Self-respect in the workplace

Knowing how to tread carefully at the workplace is essential if we are to retain our personal integrity.

Megan's letter

I joined my firm six months ago. One girl called Ruth took me under her wing. One evening Ruth confessed to doing something stupid at work. She became so tearful that, in the spirit of empathy, I told her about a relationship mistake I'd made at my last company. A few days later, my boss called me in and advised me to stay away from Ruth as she was the office gossip, known as Radio Ruth. I'm now mortified in case my new boss knows about what I did at my last company. I also keep thinking my colleagues are looking at me differently. What on earth can I do? I don't want to leave so soon after joining, but I don't know how to face my colleagues.

Regards, Megan

In her acute embarrassment, Megan wants to disappear or become invisible. This is the impulse lying behind her internal debate about whether to leave the company. In her agony, she imagines that her colleagues know everything about her, that she's been stripped bare – that's how exposed she feels.

It's probably a good sign that Megan's boss gave her the heads up about Ruth's gossiping tendencies. It suggests that few people are impressed by it and would prefer to protect Megan. But Megan needs to explore what has happened in this situation, and whether it can tell her anything useful about herself. For example, despite feeling confident about winning the new job, once she started at the firm Megan found herself behaving like a helpless victim, needing to be rescued. This in turn played right into the hands of someone like Ruth who needs people to rescue.

Ruth is the kind of person at work who doesn't have true friends. She makes herself feel validated and part of the group by 'feeding' colleagues gossip. This has become her role in the department and, because she conveys 'entertaining' or useful information, her colleagues are happy to have her play this role. After all, office gossips often possess information that hasn't made it through the more formal methods of work communication. So both sides in the transaction gain something.

Yet a colleague's interest in Ruth and her gossip is short-lived. Listening to gossip makes the colleague feel grubby. By not making any further attempt to include Ruth in the group, Ruth feels spurned and so she tries harder with more gossip, and so the pattern continues. With so many colleagues increasingly indifferent to Ruth, Ruth needs to find new victims to latch onto, new sources of juicy gossip – new victims like Megan.

Ruth needs Megan but Megan doesn't need Ruth. It's just that in the early days of being the Newbie, Megan took the easy option by relying too much on Ruth. Shrewdly, Megan's boss has now given Megan a wake-up call: stand on your own two feet, or risk being dragged under by Radio Ruth.

In her relationships with colleagues, Megan's priority must be to reinforce her professional integrity. She must knuckle down and perform well to earn their respect. Megan needs to demonstrate professionalism in her work relationships to eradicate any possible suspicion that she's like Ruth.

As part of this distancing from Ruth, Megan needs to avoid non-essential contact with her. This is in spite of the fact that Megan is desperate to know whether and how much Ruth has spread gossip about her. What Megan needs to focus on is what she *can* control. She can control whether she interacts with Ruth more than she needs to. And she can control how hard she works, how professional and how conscientious she is. As upsetting as this incident has been for Megan, it's a useful reminder that in the workplace, respect comes way ahead of friendship.

Regaining your integrity

If Megan's story echoes your own, and you think you might have done something to damage your integrity at work, concentrate on being professional and earning respect in the workplace by doing your job well. Distance yourself from colleagues with negative energy, even if they appear to be tolerated by others in your workplace. And accept that you can't control what others say about you. All you can control is working conscientiously enough to prove any negative impressions inaccurate.

Top Tip
Take work friendships more slowly than outside the workplace, because the options around keeping your distance are harder there than in relationships that don't impact on your employment.

The office letch

Sadly, normal codes of conduct can fly out the window at the Christmas party.

Alisa's letter

I work in a large department. Every year, ahead of the Christmas party, the men rate the Top Three Tottie among the girls, and place bets as to which men and women will snog at the disco. As a result, the men imagine they have free licence to grope us women. I've tried to take it in good spirits, as I don't want to be labelled a party-pooper or to have it re-bound on me at appraisal time, but actually it disgusts me. And that's despite having come second in last year's ranking, for which I was meant to feel flattered! Should I speak up, or am I doing my chances of promotion zero good at all?

Regards, Alisa

The power of the group means it's often hard, not to say almost impossible, to go against the herd. But in most companies such behaviour would now be regarded as sexual harassment, in which case Alisa's stance doesn't sound quite so party-pooperish. This may make it easier to challenge the general office response.

If the party antics only occur once a year, Alisa may decide it's not worth making a fuss, although, as she says to me, it's a shame her chance for a good boogie is spoiled. However she decides to play it, focusing on her own behaviour is essential. It might include speaking in advance of the event to other colleagues, male and female, to see how they view this tacky seasonal tradition. It might involve, on the night, giving the dance-floor sex pest a firm 'no' (as though to a dog!) and walking away to another part of the dance floor. And it might involve simply leaving the party early, boogie or no boogie. The key is that by retaining her personal integrity, Alisa maintains her self-respect.

Maintaining self-respect

If you find yourself in a similar situation to Alisa, and are confronted by unpalatable workplace rituals, remember that negotiating our way around the office is sometimes about choosing which battles to fight. I had a colleague who thoroughly disapproved that the annual office entertainment was never open to partners/ spouses. At the same time, he didn't believe it was worth creating a scene about one party when in his view there were bigger issues about how the department functioned that needed addressing, and for which he was prepared to fight fiercely. In this situation, my colleague focused on what he could address, which was his own behaviour. So when the party came around each year, he was always, 'sadly, double-booked'.

Top Tip
Given that sexual harassment is unacceptable, modelling a
fresh way of dealing with the sex pests for colleagues
might encourage others to stand up to them too.

Misreading the signs

Because we spend so much time at work, we tend to assume that
any relationships that flourish there must be friendship.

Carole's letter

*I've been at my company three years and was close to my assistant
Angela, professionally and socially. Four months ago she got a job
in a different part of the company on a different floor, and I haven't
seen her since. Now I hear she's getting married and I haven't been
invited to the wedding. In private I'm hurt, although I don't want
to make a big deal of it. I'll probably buy a gift from the wedding
list, but how could I have misread this relationship so badly?*

Regards, Carole

What Carole regards as a close friendship is weaker than she
thought. Yet throughout life, while some friendships last, there
are others that don't survive. We move away, we have kids, we
don't have kids, we change jobs. At the same time, the intensity
of the workplace throws people together who might otherwise
never meet. It can forge the most enriching, fruitful relationships.
Meeting through work the person we go on to marry is a familiar
scenario for many couples.

But Carole may have mistaken office civility and harmony for genuine friendship. So I ask Carole to assess her feelings. She feels sad at the ending of something and is desperate to regain it. The plan to buy a wedding present may be a warm gesture of generosity. It may be a way to cling on to the friendship. It may even be an unconscious way to try to make Angela feel guilty. Carole needs to examine why the friendship meant so much to her.

Carole's father was a diplomat. As a child, Carole changed schools many times. The ending with Angela presses a painful button for Carole about keeping friends, and whether she's to blame for not staying in touch with people. Carole sees she has a tendency to blame herself if friendships go awry. In asking whether she's misread the friendship signs with Angela, she beats herself up that it's her fault. Challenging such negative thoughts is hard, but it can be done consciously. It also helps to develop a sense of perspective. Not all work relationships survive separation, because some are based more on proximity.

We're all made uncomfortable by endings and separations, so it's possible that the ending with Angela has prompted Carole to elevate the relationship from colleague to friend. However, with a new job and an engagement, Angela sounds like she's been busy. She might not be the close friend Carole imagined, but she may still be fond of Carole and pleased for the relationship to continue. At some stage, it would be appropriate for Carole to make contact, perhaps to invite Angela for a celebratory drink.

Reality check

If Carole's situation resonates for you, and you wonder whether you've misread a relationship at work, have compassion for your feelings that something you've valued has changed or gone. Understand that the intense setting can also mask the reality of the situation; if you weren't sitting in adjoining cubicles, or working on a particular project, you wouldn't necessarily be friends with this person you see on a daily basis. Also, take the time to seek out new friends so as not to be so reliant on one person.

Top Tip
It's hard sometimes to distinguish between work intimacy and proper friendship. Don't blame yourself if at work friendships fade, but understand that there's a natural shift of office dynamics, where people move on to be replaced by new folk.

Coping with the new (ar)rival

Arriving in a company forces us to adapt to the new environment, but having someone new arrive at our existing place of work also requires some negotiation.

Sandrine's letter

I've worked at the same school for five years, and am now head of department. However, we now have a new deputy head of the whole school, and he's ruffled feathers from the start. He has a grand vision about how we could change our approach and is always peeling staff away for 'little chats' to suggest new ways of working. The headmaster obviously thinks the man is wonderful and suggests we all listen to his new ideas. In the staff room we try to make light of it, but deep down we're annoyed. What can we do without coming across like the stroppy adolescents we teach?

Regards, Sandrine

The arrival of a new member of staff into an organization is similar to the arrival in a family of a new baby. While the baby is a source of great joy to many, it also changes the dynamics between the parents and is a rival for parental attention for any siblings. In other words, new members of staff have to do very little to ruffle at least someone's feathers. So I ask Sandrine to explore what emotions this new grouping brings up for her.

She's surprised by how many separate emotions she can name, including resentment, hostility, and even fear that she might lose her job. What we see is how uncertainty and the unknown can take us right back to primitive emotions, as though our very survival is at stake.

By being reluctant to fall in with the headmaster's suggestion to listen to the new deputy head's 'vision', Sandrine is trying to stay in an old, familiar place, where things are done in the old way. We explore how listening doesn't have to mean 'agreeing with' or even 'implementing'. Looked at in this way, listening is simply giving someone a chance to be heard. Sandrine understands that her resistance to this new Other, 'The Newbie', is about her fear of being rejected. That somehow if the deputy head's new vision is adopted, then maybe this means the old way, which included her, was bad or past its sell-by-date.

Having listened to the new ideas, Sandrine is in a better position to put forward her own suggestions or alternatives. This means she comes across less like one of the adolescents they all teach, and more like an engaged, committed member of staff who has the best interests of the school and its future at heart.

Coping with new arrivals

If Sandrine's story resonates for you, and there's a new person in your workplace, list the different emotions this arrival has brought up in you, and don't be surprised at how strong some of these feelings are. Like a child faced with the arrival of a baby in the family, the arrival of this new member of staff may have knocked your confidence. Use the situation to become more engaged and pro-active in your workplace, which will also reinvigorate your confidence.

Top Tip

Give the new person the benefit of the doubt and hear what they have to say; you don't have to agree with them, but at the same time, respond with your own ideas and alternatives and see their arrival as an energizing opportunity for you.

Setting boundaries

The workplace, like any gathering of people, is a jumble of personalities. But unlike in many other groups, cooperation in the workplace is crucial, where getting along with people at work is linked to ongoing employment. Good relationships in the workplace can transform an otherwise unfulfilling job.

Yet whether we like our colleagues or not, setting boundaries is vital. Being part of a group doesn't mean we must lose our sense of our individuality. For example, changing the subject when a colleague starts bitching about another colleague or wants to pass on salacious gossip is a polite way of showing that you don't respect such behaviour.

You also need to set the boundary by speaking out if you have a colleague who takes all the credit for something you've done. This is about asserting your right to be known as having worked on a deal or a project or a task. In that moment, being seen as having worked on that job is part of your identity in the workplace and, if others choose to steal this aspect of your identity, you must reclaim it. It's also worth thinking about refusing to work with that person again unless credit can be guaranteed in advance. As I say elsewhere, it's helpful to be the cheerleader for our team of one.

Setting a boundary also means having the courage to say 'no' to new tasks when you're already too busy. Many of us fear saying no will suggest a lack of commitment. Some of us are people-pleasers and don't want to incur someone's negativity by saying something they don't want to hear. But saying no when you're overloaded shows bosses you possess self-respect and that you want your work to remain at a high standard rather than taking on too much and letting people down.

Lastly, setting a boundary is also important when dealing with colleagues who delegate too much and try to dump their work on us or others. Setting the boundary, politely yet firmly, will stop such behaviour from this particular Other and give you more time to do your own work properly.

In times of economic insecurity and a shrinking job market, the old option of handing in your notice if you find the workplace unpleasant is not as feasible. This makes getting on with your colleagues even more vital. Work relationships and career politics can be complex, but paying attention to your own behaviour and maintaining our own integrity can only strengthen our identity at work. This can positively affect how you view yourself in the workplace, which in turn increases your self-esteem. In a funny way, even annoying work-ships can be the making of you.

CHAPTER 9
Social Media

The big question for the twenty-first century has become: is social media simply a harmless global cocktail party, a sort of social snack, or is it rapidly promoting emotional prostitution?

The upsides

When emails, texts, Facebook, and Twitter first exploded onto our consciousness, they were heralded as tools that might facilitate fulfilling relationships. And, in some ways, they've had very positive influences on how we conduct and maintain relationships. We can remain in regular touch with people all over the world, in different time zones, and leading radically different lives to ourselves. And if and when we do meet up, we're completely up to speed with each other's lives and can plunge straight into a deeper connection.

We can find like-minded souls who share our passions for cupcakes or antiques, and join in passionate conversations on blogs. We can follow live sporting events on Twitter and, as well as shouting at the referee from our armchair, can tweet a critique that might be read out on the radio or posted on an Internet stream. If we like a book (such as this one!), we can contact the author on Twitter. We can post comments to articles appearing in publications across the globe, from Lima to Laos. Instead of putting off phoning someone because we fear not having anything significant to say right now, we can drop them a text, or post on their Facebook wall, which is the equivalent of saying 'hi' to someone in the street or office corridor.

Even if the contact is brief, it's still contact. And for some relationships this is sufficient. And for those relationships where we're determined not to let geography and time zones impede development, Skype and FaceTime now allow for virtual face-to-face communication. Who on earth would want to go back to the days where letters took weeks to arrive and we'd never met anyone from another village let alone another continent.

We can even meet our partners now online. When two people eventually meet, they already have important things in common and have shared their views. Devotees say it takes the pressure off the 'old system' of blind dates and practising chat-up lines in the bathroom mirror, and increases the chances that couples actually have a friendship to start with, based on shared interests.

The downsides

And yet social media, in all its gorgeous complexity and sophistication, has also massively increased the relationship complications. Our relationship skills are weakening or becoming stunted. We can hide behind social media accounts and avatars to avoid having authentic one-to-one relationships with the real people in our lives. We can inhabit virtual worlds and orchestrate outcomes, leaving us frustrated with our lack of control or excitement in the real world. And our ability to read non-verbal cues such as body language, micro-gestures or facial expressions may be diminished, seriously compromising our ability to negotiate real-life encounters when they arise.

Virtual relationships

We're becoming so attuned to half-lives and non-reality that we might not recognize an unfulfilling or inappropriate relationship when it invades our space.

Janine's letter

I'm thirty-four. Last year I met Daniel in a bar and even though we live two hundred miles apart, we saw each other on and off for about six months. We texted each other every day and I stored all his texts in a separate folder on my phone. When Daniel sent me a text saying it was all over, I found it really hard to accept. He does reply to my requests to meet up but he's been very distant, taking ages to return my texts at all. In my head I know the relationship is over but I just can't get over him. What can I do?

Regards, Janine

Janine's relationship was based on texts and sex, but it felt at the time both complete and fulfilling. Texts give both the sender and the receiver an illusion of intimacy. Janine's relationship felt real enough because there was daily text contact, in the modern way. But over time she and I have looked back at how little substance the relationship actually possessed. There was very little texture to it, few shared experiences, little depth, little growth. There was lots of fantastic sex and, oh yes, all those texts. Including the one announcing the break-up.

The problem is, texts are scarily easy to send. Texting colludes with our inner child, which has very poor impulse control. Sometimes we don't even type words, we simply BBM emoticons. They do say a picture paints a thousand words, and I'd definitely agree with regard to a Titian painting or a Doisneau photograph, but I have my doubts when the image in question is a yellow Smiley face wearing sunglasses.

So the work Janine and I do is twofold: getting her to examine the relationship as a prelude for moving on healthily from the break-up; and exploring the ways in which she's using the texts in the folder as a barrier to actually moving on. This is hard because for Janine the 'folder' of texts feels 'real' – it can be opened and gazed at when Janine needs comfort. And because her phone is always to hand, she can scroll through the messages with alarming frequency. When she feels anxious or sad about Daniel dumping her, she soothes herself by looking at his texts, as reassuring as if he's there – perhaps more so.

In this way, she's behaving like an infant who needs a dummy to feel soothed, or an addict who needs a 'fix' reading the texts to survive her anxiety. She's no longer in a relationship with Daniel, but she is *still* in a relationship with his texts. It takes her six months to get to a place where she can delete the folder completely.

Facing reality and letting go

If Janine's story echoes yours, and you can't stop reading a lover's texts or stalking their profile on Facebook, you can try going 'cold turkey', by de-friending your ex on Facebook, taking time out from using Facebook completely so that you don't get to see all your other friends' interactions with your ex, and deleting their texts. Understand that although the 'contact' feels real, it's un-helpfully contributing to the fantasy that your ex is still somehow in your life, which is making it harder to 'let go'. Keep a diary of your emotions to identify the link between your mood and your urge to check your phone.

Top Tip
Pursue other activities to wean yourself off your attachment to your phone or Facebook/Twitter accounts, and maybe instigate a social media 'amnesty' to create several hours a day when you don't use social media.

Our inner narcissist

Another downside of social media is that it taps into our craving for positive affirmation. In this age of YouTube, we want to be seen and adored. The seductive adrenalin rush we feel when people accept our Facebook request to be friends or Follow us on Twitter is similar to when people in real life pay us a compliment. It flatters our ego. However, when this high evaporates, *as it always does*, we feel compelled to contact ever more remote individuals or tweet increasingly outrageous comments to increase our visible tally of friends or followers.

We don't even have to speak to these 'friends', let alone meet up. The emotional intimacy one might expect to enjoy with family or good mates is denied, even subverted. And taken too far, it can fuel our inner narcissist, which demands constant attention. We become hungry for praise from any source.

This temporarily inflates our sense of our own talents and achievements. It generates unreal expectations about how to function in the world, or where to find authentic approval or intimacy. And it leads to disappointment when we don't achieve positive feedback.

Dipti's letter

I'm twenty-eight and came out of a long relationship about nine months ago. A friend suggested I try Internet dating and although I was sceptical, I joined up. At first it seemed great fun. I loved the fact that I could be bubbly and flirtatious online with many men, and it boosted my ego when men clicked on my profile picture and got talking. But every time I met a man, he just wanted sex. Am I misreading the signals?

Regards, Dipti

With the 'liking' of profiles and the opportunity to email before meeting, we can get past first base without even realizing it. No wonder we keep hearing stories about men who assumed sex was on the cards after all this faffing around, chatting online. Women adore the wooing and the heady sense of being pursued, whereas men can become angry at what they regard as game-playing. Again, these dissonant expectations may exist if you meet someone you fancy in real life first, it's just that social media accelerates the process.

My advice to Dipti is to be careful about the signals she might be giving out by being too flirty, too available. She must respect herself and protect herself online as much as she would in the real world.

Personal boundaries

If Dipti's experience echoes yours, and you've found yourself in difficult situations because of your interactions online, practise being cautious about giving out too much personal information online. Accept that the process is exciting but take breaks during your Internet communications so that you're less likely to get carried away.

Top Tip

As with all meetings with people we don't know at all, always tell someone else that you're meeting up, and tell them where you're going. For added security, keep your phone on.

Internet isolation

Having many Facebook or Twitter followers or fans of our MySpace or Flikr pages or views of our YouTube video makes us feel validated. 'I have this many friends,' we say to ourselves, 'which means I'm worth this much.' The trouble is, this apparent validation comes from external sources, not a secure internal one, and as a result is ephemeral and unhealthy. For people with fragile egos, such competitiveness is disastrous. The Followers, the clicks to 'like', the Re Tweeters, can tail off or move on to more exciting subjects, leaving us bereft.

Martin's letter

I worry that I'm depressed. I work on my computer from home and rarely go out, ordering my food from the supermarket online. I play online games until around three in the morning and am constantly checking my status updates. When my mother died earlier this year, it upset me at her funeral to think that I won't have anyone come to mine. How can I change?

Regards, Martin

Martin has shut down. His contact with the world is only virtual. Apart from the supermarket delivery man, he has little or no live human interaction. At our one meeting he avoided any eye contact and sat hunched in the chair, arms folded, jiggling his legs. Until his mother's death he was content with this virtual existence. It was the norm for him. So it was only by being forced into the real world, for his mother's funeral, that he was reminded about things like companionship and support and live music and the smell of flowers.

The impulse for this book is the idea that we all struggle with certain relationships. But for some people that struggle is so painful, so long-standing, that the Internet seems to provide a magic form of self-medication. We hide from the world, and in hiding, make the problem worse.

Martin is like an addict, addicted to his computer. 'The Other' in his life is the world online. But his situation is tricky in that his computer also provides his modest livelihood, so cutting off all contact is impossible. Martin's situation is therefore less like urging an alcoholic to give up booze and more like encouraging someone with an eating disorder to develop a healthier relationship with food.

I suggested Martin try graduated exposure to the outside world, such as going to a shop instead of obtaining groceries online. However, a plan to meet up with people Martin has 'met' online seemed too daunting to him. Martin's self-esteem was extremely poor, due to his depression and low self-worth because he was overweight. The only thing that seemed to work was my suggestion of a daily walk somewhere. He wouldn't need to be with anyone, but he'd be getting fresh air and exercise. The 'feel-good' endorphins released during exercise can be very good at tackling depression.

Above all, Martin was very scared of the world and of the people in it. Bullied at school, the Internet provided the perfect hermit's retreat. I didn't hear from Martin for over two years. And then one day I got an email (no surprise there, maybe) in which he told me he was feeling much better, that he'd lost three stone by 'going for walks, and buying apples in shops', and that he now has a voluntary job helping in a library, where he loves looking up books for people on the computer.

Joining the real world

If you live like Martin, and you spend a large part of your day or night online, or have reduced your circle of real live friends, start by making a point of leaving your home everyday to get fresh air and alternative stimulation. Write down the feelings you have when you think about meeting people in real life, to understand why you have retreated from the world. Work on your own self-esteem, which will help you to feel more confident at the thought of meeting people, and devise a programme of exercise for the well-being benefits it brings.

Top Tip
Build up your social exposure gradually, by having one conversation a week with a real person, for example a shopkeeper.

Fabrication

It can be nerve-wracking meeting new people, but on social media sites we lose our inhibitions. We become impulsive, and say anything to make ourselves look good. Above all we feel we must prove to others, but especially to ourselves, that we're wonderful. We're terrified of being lonely, or of being seen to lead an ordinary life.

This can lead to a deep personal dissatisfaction. It's a hugely narcissistic way of functioning in the world, and plays havoc when we actually try to forge a meaningful relationship with someone real.

Greg's letter

I've got myself into a nightmare situation because I've been lying on Facebook and on Internet chat-rooms. In the course of great conversations over many months I managed to slip in things like

*having a girlfriend when I don't, and that she and I were doing
wonderful things together like going to Amsterdam – even though
I've never been to Amsterdam. I've now become good friends with
a few people on a site, and we've planned to meet up. There's even
one girl I like and she'll be there, too. So what do I do, especially
when they ask about 'Emma', my 'girlfriend'? Even if I say we
broke up, I'm terrified they'll find out eventually.*

Regards, Greg

The creation of the fictional Emma gave Greg confidence at
a time when he was trying to make new friends. It reminds me
of women who invent 'a husband' or wear a ring when travelling alone, to ward off unwanted attention. Not too much harm
done, you might think, but lying in this way can become a
habit.

I'm not suggesting Greg wouldn't have lied in face-to-face conversations, it's just that *the isolation and detachment of our social
media exchanges make lying so much easier.* It's so much easier nowadays to manipulate our lives to become air-brushed versions of
ourselves (perfect specimens, polished and attractive), images
which in the real world are almost impossible to live up to.

An online identity is only ever a partial construct and, as Greg
now sees (and this holds good in all our relationships), one lie
may seem insignificant at the time, but it can spiral out of control.
All relationships require honesty and trust.

Greg's dilemma highlights how fickle and artificial social media
can be. A lot of the attachments aren't real. And because so many
of the lives we see on Facebook and Twitter and Flikr can be
photo-shopped or air-brushed, our real identities can feel rather
mundane or inadequate in comparison, so we run the risk of wanting to fabricate our identity. Luckily, Greg now has the chance to
throw himself into relationships with real people and leave the
fabrications behind.

Being authentic

If you're in a similar situation to Greg, and you've been fabricating your life online, examine your motives for such distortions. It's possible that you're so keen to form attachments that you've lost sight of the implications of being misleading in the real world. Did you portray a better version of yourself or have you completely misrepresented yourself?

Either way, the key is to catch yourself in the moment of lying and make a choice to communicate differently. Be your own inner adviser and warn yourself not to be so daft when about to type something misleading or untruthful. This way you can respect the real you.

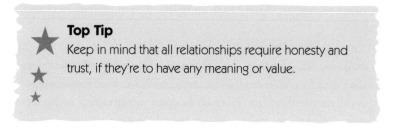

Top Tip
Keep in mind that all relationships require honesty and trust, if they're to have any meaning or value.

Setting boundaries

The relative anonymity and detachment of communicating on-line means that the boundaries we learned when growing up have weakened. When we're little, the grown-ups advise us not to say 'poo' in front of Granny, or to play with our penis in the playgroup or to have a temper tantrum at the checkout counter. This kind of boundary-setting is an essential part of good parenting and is about training the child to develop self-control and discipline. Over time, we develop this impulse control for ourselves. Social media, for all its liberation and democracy, has challenged or dismantled our ability to self-control.

Vera's letter

My husband is being contacted by a woman we both met through friends on a golfing holiday. She's a widow and on the holiday she was mugged at the airport, which left her reliant on other guests, including my husband and me. However, now we've come home, she's started sending him flirty emails and texts and even inviting him to be her golf partner. We don't know what to do. We don't want to be rude, but we can't cut her out of our lives as we share many mutual friends stretching back decades. Yet neither of us is comfortable with this woman's behaviour.

Regards, Vera

As with all relationships, setting boundaries is important, even if only in our own mind. In this case, Vera and her husband must ignore the woman's texts and emails completely. This is because even if we convince ourselves that the wording in any reply is not echoing the flirtatiousness, the other person is often in a very different space, especially in their head. They have convinced themselves that a real, mutual relationship exists, and they're usually spectacularly deaf or blind to evidence to the contrary.

In Vera's case, there's a high risk of embarrassing a possibly lonely woman, who may not mean to be flirty, or who is disinhibited because of the detachment of texting and emails. As in negotiating our way around many relationship conflicts with The Other, the method decided upon is for Vera and her husband to set their own boundary instead of trying to get the woman to change her inappropriate behaviour. In most cases, any sustained lack of response will see the communication fizzle out, so the plan is to send no replies whatsoever.

Vera and her husband also draft a joint reply stating that they both want the communication to stop, but thankfully it never gets to that awkward stage of needing to be so explicit.

Setting boundaries

If you're in a similar situation to Vera and her husband, and some-one is contacting you inappropriately, you need to set your own boundary rather than try to persuade the other person to change. Even a well-phrased response from you, which is clearly giving the brush off, runs the risk of being misconstrued. Your recipient may convince him or herself that *any* reply from you is proof that you're a willing participant in the communication. From this, they imagine they've been given the green light to continue. This is a mild variation on cyber bullying, which I address later, but it can still be upsetting and stressful, so take it seriously and main-tain your boundary.

Top Tip
Back up any boundary you set, such as not replying at all, by being consistent, as though parenting a child.

Internet porn

Sometimes our immersion in the online world runs the risk of de-stabilizing our real relationships. The increased accessibility of hardcore porn, for example, has led to a rise in people com-pulsively surfing the net, risking their relationships, even their careers. Where once boys would snigger over a copy of *Playboy* as part of their sexual education, now even pre-teens have access to disturbing, violent, and disrespectful images at a time when they're otherwise sexually ignorant and impressionable.

Kendra's letter

I'm nineteen and my boyfriend Leo is twenty-four. He's not my first sexual partner, but he's the first one who wants me to do things I'm not comfortable with. I think I might be starting to have an eating disorder because Leo is not happy with my body and he's always texting me videos saying we should try stuff. Am I abnormal for not wanting to do what he wants me to do?

Regards, Kendra

Teenage boys and girls can nowadays access scenes of sexual violence on their mobile phones, and so this warped material becomes their template for future sexual relationships. Girls imagine they have to be submissive and have perfect bodies. Boys imagine they have permission to be sexually violent and to find female pubic hair abnormal. Both sexes are influenced to believe caring sex and intimacy is dull and boring. Both sexes are destined to be sexually disillusioned and unfulfilled.

Kendra's dilemma is not new. For centuries women have often felt pressurized to be more sexually adventurous than they feel comfortable with. Yet research has shown that even limited exposure to porn changes male and female attitudes towards sex and towards their partners. Boys develop their sexual template from images and therefore porn warps their view of what is appropriate. Girls see being a porn star as an ideal similar to being a movie star or a successful reality TV contestant; in all cases, the girl is turning herself into an object to be stared at.

Kendra has a boundary in her head, a line she's not comfortable crossing, but it's coming under external pressure – not just from Leo, but from an increasing sexually saturated society and from social media that normalizes sexually disturbed behaviour and makes disturbing images as accessible as a bag of chips.

We identify what sexual behaviour is acceptable for Kendra. She also writes down a wish list of attributes in a sexual partner.

Top of her list is a boyfriend who respects her. We look at ways for Kendra to boost her self-esteem and self-respect, since *it's hard for someone to respect us when we don't respect ourselves.*

We also explore her eating issues. Kendra keeps a mood diary for a month, which helps her monitor her emotions linked to wanting to overeat. When she becomes stressed or feels inadequate (usually after a conversation about sex with Leo), she feels compelled to binge eat.

One of Kendra's fears is that Leo will dump her for being dull, with a secondary fear that he will then gossip about her, saying she's frigid. Once I've established that Leo has never actually called Kendra frigid, I work with Kendra on this projection coming from herself that by refusing certain sexual requests she's frigid. Over time we explore the idea that standing up for yourself and what you believe in sexually is a sign you won't be pushed around, and that this can bring you respect internally and externally. Kendra wept when imagining that one day her younger step-sister, Preena, aged nine, would be asked to perform similar sexual tasks for a man.

Trying to see herself as a role model for Preena gives Kendra the additional strength to reject Leo's requests, and to feel more relaxed about the fear that he might dump her for this. As Kendra talks to me and becomes more assertive in life, she becomes more assertive in her relationship with Leo. At first Leo is unsure how to handle this 'newer' Kendra and they separate for a month. During this time apart, Leo examines his own attitudes to sex and to women. Yet when Leo gets back in touch with Kendra to see if she wants to resume the relationship, Kendra tells him that for now she wants to be friends, not lovers. In her mind, she's prepared to wait for a man who respects her more than Leo currently knows how to.

Respecting sexual boundaries

If Kendra's story resonates for you, and you're coming under pressure to perform sexually in a way that is uncomfortable for you, understand that it's your body and that you get to decide what pleasure you have with it. Identify your sexual boundaries and nourish your self-respect so that you feel strong about standing up for what you believe in sexually.

Also identify if you've developed other behaviours around being pressurized to do sexual things, such as finding comfort in eating, drinking, stealing or lying. Talking to a good friend can help you feel supported when you feel under pressure from other people.

Top Tip
Keep in mind that if someone wants to dump you for saying no to certain things, they aren't worthy of you and your body.

Crackberry addiction

Something as innocuous as our mobile or smart phone can cause serious rifts in relationships. Reaching for it before greeting loved ones in the morning means the balance has tipped away from real intimacy. Partners grow incensed to see loved ones scrolling through their messages during dinner parties, wedding ceremonies, on the beach, even during conversations. At the very least, such behaviour is rude. When it occurs every day of every week of every month, this is the sign of a problem, what the media has dubbed a crackberry addiction.

Matt's letter

There are three of us in this marriage and the third 'person' is my wife's Blackberry. We both have good yet demanding jobs and, at first, this was an exciting aspect of our relationship. Neither of us is ready to settle down and have kids, but at this rate we won't even have the time to have sex. When we went away for a week recently, my wife spent all day on her phone which receives emails too, which meant neither of us could relax. My sister suggested that maybe my wife and I should see a counsellor, but my wife refused, saying she didn't have time! Her affair with her phone means there's less time for us. What can I do?

Regards, Matt

Matt's situation is an increasingly common one. It's possible that only Matt is conscious there's a problem in his relationship. It's also possible that his wife is aware too, but that her way of coping is to retreat into her work and phone to avoid painful truths. But until they can sit down and communicate about this, there can be no progress.

I get Matt to look at what attracted him to his wife initially and to explore what he wants from a marriage. He'd liked that they were both busy and successful. It made him feel like they were a power couple. Unfortunately, one of the things that drew him to her is now the very cause of his anxiety.

Because Matt is in business himself, I ask him how he manages his 'phone-time'. He has a rule to ignore his phone between 8 am and 8 pm. Together we draft a proposal about what he wants to achieve in his discussions with his wife and, looking longer term, where he sees the marriage heading. Even though he is married, he needs to be assertive about his own needs and desires within the couple.

Blackberry protocol

If you're in a similar situation to Matt, and your partner is apparently unable to function without their phone or computer, sit down with them and explain how it feels to compete with a phone, as though there's a rival in the relationship. Discuss developing a phone protocol with your partner, so that the phone is out of bounds from, say, 8 pm until 8 am.

If you think you may be addicted to your own phone, or if your partner has raised the subject with you, ask yourself what you imagine will happen if you don't answer messages superpromptly. Who do you fear being rejected by (client, boss, friend)? Or do you secretly long to feel indispensible? If you feel anxious when you're away from your phone, you may need to think about exploring those emotions, instead of using your phone as a crutch.

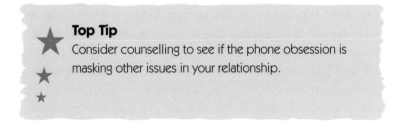

Top Tip
Consider counselling to see if the phone obsession is masking other issues in your relationship.

Trolling

A deeply troubling aspect of social media is the rise of Trolling, which is the posting of offensive or defamatory or harrassing messages on social media sites This means we can be adversely affected by people we've never met and who are not in a real relationship to us:

Sophie's letter

I'm twenty years old and I've been cyber-bullied since I was seventeen. I've tried ignoring the tweets and I've closed down my

Facebook account. Yet this has added to my sadness, as it's now harder to stay in touch with some of my friends. It's making me so miserable and I've lost loads of weight. What can I do?

Regards, Sophie

After some landmark legal cases, legislation has been introduced to make it easier for the victims of Trolling to discover their tormentor's identity. And in an ideal world we'd all have sufficient resilience, what we call Ego strength, to ignore or laugh at or dismiss or delete such contact. We might call this a 'sticks and stones' approach, as in 'sticks and stones may break my bones but words can never hurt me.'

But as Sophie has discovered, such words, especially the constant drip, drip of such words, written down, can hurt or undermine us. One of my clients who is in the public eye told me that he doesn't ever believe what the Trolls write to him, but they put him in a bad mood for the rest of the day. The mental anguish from violent, obscene, insulting, homophobic, racist, sexist, pornographic, threatening, expletive-ridden or malicious messages is very real.

Sophie's misery and weight loss point to why Trolling must be taken seriously. Some people argue that Trolling is simply free speech, but my view is that cyber-bullying creates a dangerously grey area where free speech becomes abuse or offence. And of course abuse and offence are very subjective. One person's mild offence is another person's abuse. Yet I worry that Trolls are able to hide behind the cloak of 'free speech' to continue their intimidation.

With Sophie we strengthen her sense of self, which in any case is often fragile in adolescence when we are exploring our identity. We also create a new Facebook page, one for close, carefully vetted friends only. This makes Sophie feel empowered, to see that the Trolls haven't won by taking away her friends. She explains to these friends about the Trolling and about how if it starts again they are not to respond. People who Troll are like children, craving attention from Mummy. So the best practice is not to give it to them.

Tackling the Trolls

If Sophie's experience echoes your own, and you're the target of Trolling, literally ignore what they send by not reading it. You do not need to read it, but they need to get a rise out of you in order to feel real or worthy or validated, so don't make it easy for them. Instead, work on your self-esteem by focusing on people and activities that give you pleasure. With greater Ego strength you have a greater chance of being able to laugh off or withstand their intimidation.

Top Tip

Do not reply to Trolls. If you think you're about to reply, get up and do something else (listen to music, phone a friend) until the urge passes.

Healthy social media protocol

Like proper clinical addictions, it's hard to admit that our relationship to social media might be dysfunctional. We know in the twenty-first century that people can be addicted to alcohol, drugs, shopping, gambling or sex. We understand that sometimes this is a way for us to manage our emotions, or to bury painful thoughts or memories. Addictive behaviour can be a way to make us feel good about ourselves, or to feel more in control – of ourselves or of others. And yet our attachment to social media, to our smart phones, our laptops, our Facebook page or Twitter feed, can be just as compulsive, just as hard to break.

And, taken to extremes, social media can give us the illusion of connection where none exists. Sites glorifying suicide or anorexia give the impression of providing a supportive community but this intimacy is an illusion. Its members, unlike true friends, wouldn't know us if we passed them in the street and they do not have our best interests at heart. Isolation is a key component in people contemplating suicide and secrecy is a key aspect of eating disorders. Both these traits are exacerbated by the Internet.

The key to using and not being used by The Other of social media is, as in most relationships, balance. We need to use it sparingly, as an enhancement to relationships and not as a substitute. My worry is that our compulsion for social media is some form of compensation for an inner emptiness, and I speak as someone who uses Twitter most days. I've communicated with some terrific people through Twitter, often meeting them subsequently *in person*, if you can believe in something so quaint and unfashionable. Through Twitter and Facebook I've attended events and discovered information. I've followed breaking news stories, or had a good giggle at a video that has gone viral. And when you work mainly alone as I do, such communication feels like a valuable resource for staying sane and connected.

But even I try not to Tweet or use Facebook at weekends, and smile when I catch myself getting twitchy about not using it – a sure sign that I'm suffering withdrawal-type symptoms! I know that if I wasn't on social media I'd be doing something else. Something dull, maybe, like ironing (please don't Tweet me about how much you like ironing; there's no pleasure in ironing, unless it's something simple, like pillow-cases). Or something nurturing, like refilling the bird-feeder. Or healthy, like going for a walk.

All generations can gain an enormous amount from social media. Yet we'd do well to remember that 'connecting' is never the same as 'communicating'. Yes, online contact can generate offline connections. Yet we need to be alert for how we're using social media, how often, and why, because social media tempts us to invest too much time in our 'virtual' friends and activities at the expense of the unique and precious wonderfulness of our real ones.

Notes

Chapter 2

1   In April 2007, the Centre for Longitudinal Studies noted that 'A THIRD of female university graduates born in 1970 will never have children by 2015.'

Chapter 7

1   *Children of Divorced Couples*, The Office for National Statistics (December 2011).

Useful Resources

MIND
www.mind.org.uk
A mental health charity, offering advice and support for anyone with a mental health issue, including a superb legal advice line on **0300 466 6463.**

UKCP
www.psychotherapy.org.uk
A national register of psychotherapists and psychotherapeutic counsellors who meet exacting standards and training requirements. Has a user-friendly Find a Therapist option.

Refuge and Women's Aid
www.refuge.org.uk and www.womensaid.org.uk
Both charities are linked to the 24-hour freephone National Domestic Violence helpline on **0808 2000 247.**

Headspace
www.getsomeheadspace.com
Making meditation simple, with a free 10-day trial online.

***Psychologies* magazine**
www.psychologies.co.uk
The women's glossy magazine for people who are life curious.

The Complete Idiot's Guide to Tantric Sex
By Dr. Judy Kuriansky, published by Alpha
An informative and user-friendly guide to sensual intimacy.

Index